# Concrete Architecture
## Design and Construction

# Concrete Architecture
## Design and Construction

**Burkhard Fröhlich (ed.)**

DBZ Deutsche BauZeitschrift
Gütersloh

Birkhäuser – Publishers for Architecture
Basel · Boston · Berlin

# Contents

# Concrete Keywords

The most important standard for the production and use of concrete and reinforced concrete, in Germany DIN 1045, was replaced in 2000 at European Level by EN 206-1 "Concrete – performance, production, placing and compliance criteria". In Germany this is complemented and defined more precisely for national applications in DIN 1045-2 "...to DIN EN 206-1". The rules on the design were also revised in DIN 1045-2, the construction of concrete and reinforced concrete were revised in DIN 1045-3 and the production of precast concrete components in DIN 1045-4.

DIN EN 197-1 has considerably increased the number of standardised cements. However, it does not include cements with special properties that, above all, are more important at a national level. In Germany these continue to be covered by DIN 1164.

Editor: Burkhard Fröhlich
Co-Editor: Sonja Schulenburg

Texts: Martin Möllmann (8), Till Wöhler (12, 56), Enrico Santifaller (18, 52), Michael Brüggemann, (23), Renate Strobel (24), Heinrich Hochthaler (30), Anke Wöhler (36), Annika Knudsen (40), Christine Ryll (46), Ulrike Meywald (57, 58), Dirk Forberger (60), Herbert Hendrichs (62), Winfried Hamel, Erich Limpens (64), Thomas Schrepfer (66), Günter Ruffert (70),
Markus Koschenz, EMPA/Swiss Federal Laboratories for Materials Testing and Research (74), Bjarne W. Olesen (77)

English translation: Robin Benson, Berlin
English copy-editing: Donald Nicholson-Smith

Photographs: Dyckerhoff AG, Wiesbaden (8, 9,10), Friedrich Busam, Berlin (8), Torben Eskerod, Kopenhagen (12, 13, 15, 16, 17,), Dietmar Strauß, Besigheim (18, 19, 20, 21, 22) Beckenhaub+Hohm, Bad König (23) Peter Bonfig, München (24, 25, 27, 29), Peter Oszvald, Bonn (30, 31, 32, 33, 34, 35), Javier Azurmendi, Madrid (36, 37, 38, 39), Dorfmüller + Kröger, Hamburg (40, 41, 42, 43, 44, 45), Carl Lang, Denkendorf (46, 47, 48, 49, 50, 51) Werner Kalgofsky, Wien (52, 53, 54, 55), Roland Halbe/ artur, Köln(56), Thomas Flechtner, © Kunstmuseum Liechtenstein, Vaduz (57), Fischer Architekten, Viernheim (58), Dirk Forberger, Ludwigslust (60, 61), Readymix Baustoffgruppe, Ratingen (62, 63), Thomas Schrepfer, Berlin (67, 68), Günter Ruffert, Essen (70, 71, 72, 73), EMPA/Swiss Federal Laboratories for Material Testing and Research, Dübendorf (74), Velta, Norderstedt (77)

Graphic design: Nicole Bischof, Vera Brinkkemper

This book is a cooperation project between DBZ – Deutsche BauZeitschrift and Birkhäuser – Publishers for Architecture

A CIP catalogue record for this book is available from the Library of Congress, Washington D.C., USA

Die Deutsche Bibliothek – CIP-Einheitsaufnahme

Concrete architecture : design and construction / Burkhard Fröhlich (ed.).
[Engl. transl.: Robin Benson]. - Basel ; Berlin ; Boston : Birkhäuser;
Gütersloh : Dt. BauZeitschrift, 2002
ISBN 3-7643-6872-1

© 2002 Birkhäuser – Publishers for Architecture, P.O. Box 133, CH-4010 Basel, Switzerland
Member of the BertelsmannSpringer Publishing Group
BertelsmannSpringer Bauverlag GmbH, Avenwedder Str. 55, D-33311 Gütersloh, Germany
Member of the BertelsmannSpringer Publishing Group

Printed on acid-free paper produced from chlorine-free pulp. TCF ∞
Printed in Germany
ISBN 3-7643-6872-1

9 8 7 6 5 4 3 2 1

www.dbz.de
www.birkhauser.ch

Information:

www.concrete.com
www.concrete-info.com
www.concretenetwork.com
www.worldofconcrete.com

Also available from Birkhäuser:

Bennett, David
Exploring Concrete Architecture – Tone, Texture, Form
ISBN 3-7643-6271-5

Kind-Barkauskas, Friedbert / Kauhsen, Bruno / Polònyi, Stefan / Brandt, Jörg
Concrete Construction Manual.
ISBN 3-7643-6724-5

Birkhäuser – Publishers for Architecture
Basel · Berlin · Boston

# Concrete in Architecture

Jubilee Line

# Diversity instead of Sameness

**Nowadays, architecture is inconceivable without concrete, a building material that dates back to classical antiquity. Recent examples reveal the great variety of uses to which concrete lends itself.**

Extension in seamless concrete with sandblasted surface: Swiss Embassy, Berlin
Architects: Diener + Diener, Basel

Concrete has played an important role in shaping the world, especially during the 20th century. It has proved indispensable in the extensive reconstruction work that has all too often been necessary in the wake of wars. Building materials, like building construction, have bowed to progress. In the process, the development of concrete has sometimes involved painful experiences for those responsible for constructing buildings, especially when formwork is removed, revealing poor surfaces and an awful mixture of colours underneath. In the international race among architects to build "higher, faster and further", the notions of "more beautiful and more elegant" have often been neglected. Fortunately, there have been many masterpieces, especially in recent years, demonstrating the high aesthetic standards modern building materials are capable of fulfilling. Every schoolchild is familiar with the remarkable process whereby the artificial stone known as concrete is made: a mixture of cement, sand and just a little water hardens to stone almost miraculously within a matter of hours. Not only that, the resulting stone assumes the form bestowed upon it by its creator. The skill of making and forming concrete is age-old. In antiquity, the Romans were already achieving masterful results in this field.

## Concrete Yesterday and Today

The most impressive work of engineering in classical antiquity is surely the Pantheon in Rome, a structure spanned by a dome of so-called Roman concrete (opus cementitium). The span of the dome, which was built in 120 BC, is vast, measuring 43.6 m; it was only surpassed – in 1911! – by a 65m-wide reinforced concrete dome erected for the Centenary Hall in Wroclaw. Improvements in the tensile strength of the material had meanwhile been achieved using suitable reinforcements (generally of steel). Optimised binders, especially cement systems, brought about a considerable improvement in pouring and compacting. Henceforth, it was no longer necessary to compact freshly mixed concrete by means of such noisy devices as vibrator cylinders. Modern types of concrete compact spontaneously, attaining their optimum state, as desired, in a manner that is satisfying from the point of view of structure, statics and aesthetics. Owing to its infinite pliability and colouring, concrete can be used for a greater variety of purposes than any other building material: for creating melancholic as well as euphoric moods, for restrained and modest structures, as well as for extroverted, elegant building projects. In the past, only insiders were generally in a position to implement architectural ideas in a satisfactory way. But the current economic situation is compelling the construction industry to change its structures radically, with the result that it has never before displayed such a plethora of innovative ideas. Here, then, is a unique opportunity to win over a few more friends for concrete as a building material with novel properties.

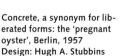

Concrete, a synonym for liberated forms: the 'pregnant oyster', Berlin, 1957
Design: Hugh A. Stubbins

## Concrete and the Quality of Life

The desire creatively to design both buildings and the surfaces of building components is no mere passing fashion. Architectural design affects the quality of life. With its almost unlimited mouldability and functionality, concrete offers creative architecture seemingly boundless possibilities. Concrete surface design can highlight, bring out or enhance the architecture of a building; alternatively, it can break building down into a wealth of detail. But it is never a substitute for the architecture itself.

As society's values and ideas have changed, the demands on building materials have changed too. Functionality alone no longer stands in the foreground. Far greater importance is attached to designing environments so that they express individuality. Building materials – both the type and quality used – also have a great influence on social aspects of life, expressing taste and bestowing social prestige.

The desire for an individually designed environment also presents a great opportunity for using concrete, a material that has been rediscovered in the past few years and also offers a myriad of possibilities. No image so aptly captures the properties of concrete as that of "flowing rock": it is firm and enduring; it allows for great variety in design; it can assume any form; and it combines the protective and functional with the creative and the aesthetic.

## Concrete and Design

Technological developments in the field of concrete have made it possible to produce strengths of >B 100. Buildings are expected to have increasingly slender cross-sections, greater spans and – because of the dimensions – ever greater load transmissions. Such requirements, in turn, place particular demands on the static properties of the building material. A close look at our environment reveals that from the objects of everyday life to our very selves, the objects surrounding us in our society have become far more colourful. And this colourfulness is now expected of building materials too. Hence, blue and pink premixed façade rendering or green and blue concrete roof tiles are no longer a rarity. Alongside concrete's good structural properties, with which we are well familiar, its aesthetic qualities are also in demand; with their demands and desires, architects are telling us that the façade, the skin, the building elements and precast concrete elements ought to be designed in accordance with individually chosen criteria.

Concrete permits a wide range of design approaches and processes, so that each building element may be given the desired appearance: the colouring of the concrete initially depends on its surface and the way it is treated. The colouring of untreated surfaces corresponds to that of the external hardened cement layer; in other words, the colour of the cement. However, when concrete surfaces are processed, this cement layer is removed, so that the colour effect is now produced by the interplay of the exposed aggregates and the hardened cement paste.

Special optical effects can also be achieved by forming, profiling and structuring the concrete surface. Shuttering lends concrete building elements specific forms which, in combination with added colour pigments, set colour accents. In addition to the above-mentioned procedures, the colouring and colour intensity of the concrete can also be determined by the choice of aggregate and compacting process. Together, all these processes help to give the concrete its individual appearance.

## Concrete and Colouring

Aggregate accounts for 80 per cent or more of the concrete mix. As a component, "aggregate" is thus critical in colouring concrete. Most aggregates are natural products: chalk, quartz, granites and porphyry. Both the colouring and the appearance of the concrete surface depend on the fineness of the aggregates used. Apart from the aggregates, the colour of the cement also determines the colour of the hardened cement paste. Standard cements come in various shades of grey. But white cements have greater design potential. White Portland cement is produced using a special raw material (with a low iron oxide content), a particular burning procedure (fuels, cooling) and, last but not least, a suitable grinding method (steels with a high alloy content). Light, hardened cement paste constitutes an ideal matrix in which coloured aggregates form a good contrast; thanks to cement's neutral colour the added dyes lend the hardened paste a clear, powerful

Structural elements in precast concrete and in situ concrete with pointed surface: Mexican Embassy, Berlin Architects: Teodoro González de León and Francisco Serrano, Mexico City

hue without producing a grey film. The desired colouring can also be produced by adding pigments to the concrete mix, these usually being synthetic, inorganic iron oxide pigments, such as cobalt blue and chromium oxide green. Industrial sources can now supply a wide range of pigments with varying, subtle shades, so that almost any intermediate colour can be reproduced from the four basic colours: black, yellow, red and white.

### Concrete and Surfaces

Concrete can be processed in a fresh, virgin or hardened state. These surface-processing techniques expose the aggregate grains to varying degrees. The colour effect of the building component is thus created by the interplay of the exposed aggregate materials and the hardened cement paste. Hence, the colour effect will also vary according to the process employed.

Over 80 per cent of their entire area, the colour of treated surfaces is determined by that of the aggregate used. The remaining surface areas of the hardened cement paste can be modified by adding fine sands and pigments, or left in their original colour around the aggregate grains. Even though these areas are very small, the colour of the cement still comes into its own (in washed-out concrete surfaces, for example), influencing the optical effect around the grains. White cement, for instance, creates a light contrast in hardened cement paste, making the colour of the embedded grains appear more radiant and intense. Grey cement, on the other hand, makes added colours appear darker.

### Concrete – a Building Material with a Future

New developments, especially in the area of process and machine technology, will significantly affect more than just the aesthetic properties of concrete in the future. The countless innovations in the field of concrete application are also generating ever more "specialities", corresponding to the increasingly differentiated requirements of site work. Such specialities include, for instance, the extremely user-friendly self-compacting concretes. These not only permit more rapid and thus more economical building construction, but also reduce the number of compacting processes, in turn reducing noise and creating a more humane and environmentally friendly work situation.

Future concretes will do away with the compacting process "spontaneously", since they will automatically compact to an optimum degree, thus fulfilling all the desired static requirements. Their extremely even surfaces will also make them look quite impressive. There will be no need to hide them beneath panelling and coats of paint as has often been the case in the past. Concretes will no longer be reserved for structural work and shaping space, they will also be used for facades and surfaces.

Changes in concrete technology will also make it possible to construct more slender buildings in the future. "More slender" means lighter architecture and thinner walls, whilst fulfilling all the customary good static requirements. This will not only offer advantages for concrete construction in the areas of assembly and transport, but also cut time and costs – decisive factors in an age in which cost considerations play a crucial role.

What next? When it comes to producing concrete and prefabricated building components, no other industrial country in the world possesses an infrastructure equalling Germany's. Architects ought to take advantage of this and make greater use of prefabricated concrete parts. Recent architecture, especially since the radical changes at the end of the 1980s, has clearly demonstrated the enormous possibilities of concrete as a building material. Architects ought to exploit this situation and deploy the new aesthetic potential of concrete, now and in the future, to find contemporary and individualised solutions to the challenges facing them.

Smooth fair-face concrete elements for facades and balconies.

**Projects**

# The New Court Building in Tarnby, Denmark

Architects: Fuglsang & Mandrup-Poulsen ApS, Kopenhagen

**Court buildings tend to inspire fear and convey severity, authority and uniformity. But this new Danish-style court building is different: it is designed to convey lightness and openness; concrete unexpectedly plays its part in this too.**

In 1997, legal proceedings in the small Danish town of Tarnby were still being held in rented rooms on a decontaminated site. To the town inhabitants, this was an intolerable state of affairs, one that could only be remedied by erecting a new building. No sooner said than done. A design competition was held in next to no time, with Niels Fuglsang and Dorte Mandrup-Poulsen from Copenhagen emerging as winners in the course of the year. At the same time, the Ministry of Justice issued guidelines on how royal Danish court buildings were to be designed in the future: more openness and an improved service to citizens – demands that were to play an important role in the implementation of this project.

## The Arrangement of the Buildings

The site was located in a suburban centre, or, to be more specific, on open ground amidst public buildings constructed during the 1960s, including a civic hall, a police station, a library and a church. With this as their starting point, the architects chose to design a free-standing sculptural composition that would act as a focal point, lending order to the surrounding buildings. To satisfy the extremely complex logistical requirements of a court, four office wings laid out in cross formation were grouped around a three-storey foyer building with high windows. Each wing houses a different court function: the secretaries' office, the courtroom, the waiting room for the litigants, the court adjacent to the court messenger's office, the records office and a canteen – all on a total area of 1,300 square metres.

## Lightness and Openness

As places where difficult and controversial matters are settled, involving the authorities and people from all walks of life, court buildings often convey an impression of authority, severity and, above all, uniformity. This particular design was intended to create a building (taking into consideration the new guidelines issued by the Ministry of Justice) which expressed both lightness and openness vis-à-vis its surroundings, yet still provided an appropriately solemn setting for the diverse legal disputes to be held there. Even from afar, the foyer building, with its 3-storey-high glass façade, suggests an inviting openness that is not at all superficial, but programmatic in nature: four courtyards have been created between the buildings and the quadratic external boundary of the property. Thus, the public areas inside the buildings all face outwards, granting both the

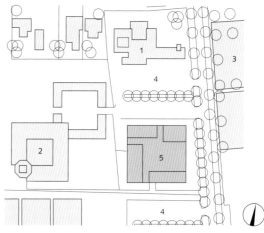

Site plan 1:2,500

1 Church
2 Police station
3 School
4 Car park
5 Law court

14

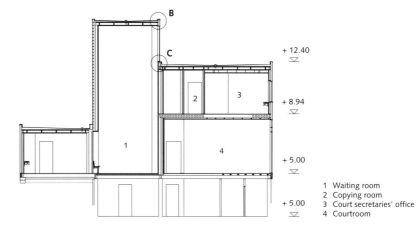

+ 12.40

+ 8.94

+ 5.00

+ 5.00

1 Waiting room
2 Copying room
3 Court secretaries' office
4 Courtroom

**Section AA 1:250**

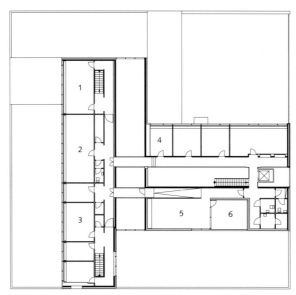

1 Judge's office
2 Court secretaries' office
3 Office
4 Copying room
5 Canteen
6 Terrace

**First floor 1:500**

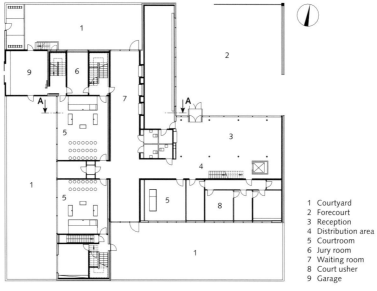

1 Courtyard
2 Forecourt
3 Reception
4 Distribution area
5 Courtroom
6 Jury room
7 Waiting room
8 Court usher
9 Garage

**Ground floor 1:500**

public and employees a good view of the outside world, letting in a great deal of natural light, and providing a vista of the gardens, without giving anyone the feeling of being on display.

## Structure

The building was executed on a low budget by several different construction companies. Hence, the primary structure comprises an inexpensive steel frame, which may surprise the observer at first sight. Despite its obviously solid appearance, the concrete does not perform a structural function; it is combined instead with LECA façade elements of lightweight aggregate concrete. (For several decades now, LECA wall elements have stood for short construction periods in Denmark.) Combining considerable dead weight with thin wall thicknesses, they provide sound insulation and possess good diffusion properties. Having an even and open structure, the surfaces are easy to treat. For this building, for example, the façades were faced with dyed stucco, creating an almost perfect impression of solid exterior walls, and thus matching the site boundary walls, which form a courtyard. The glazed façades, executed in glass and aluminium, add to the lightness radiated by the building as a whole. And even on the inside, one feels more as if one were moving around in a modern Scandinavian home than in an intimidating palace of justice demanding respect. Some of the walls in the court foyer and in the courtroom itself are clad with maple battens, a warm material covering the unattractive sound-insulating tiles. All the interior walls are executed as flexible dividing walls (plasterboard framed-partition walls) to lower the cost of any subsequent changes. Oak planks and concrete plaster were used for the floors and the public areas, which are supplied with underfloor heating. The canteens and the offices, which have linoleum flooring, are heated by radiators. Natural ventilation ensures that the air inside the courthouse is changed. However, it will take more conventional methods to clear the bad atmosphere arising in the courtroom – and will probably require the help of everyone involved in the court proceedings.

Inside, one has feels more as if one were in a modern Scandinavian home than in a court of law.

1 Aluminium/glass façade
2 Joint, elastic on the outside
3 Rigid foam plastic sheet
4 Joint, elastic on the inside
5 Stucco facing
6 100 mm concrete element
7 Mineral wool
8 50 × 100 mm wooden beams
9 Zinc capping
10 15 × 50 mm wooden lath
11 45 × 45 mm wedge-shaped insulation
12 19 mm planking
13 Roofing felt
14 45 mm mineral wool
15 2 × 13 mm plasterboard
16 25 mm mineral wool
17 45 × 16 mm wooden beam
18 30 × 30 mm wooden lath
19 Vapour seal

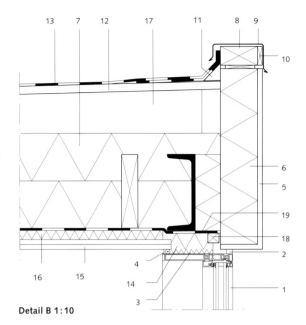

**Detail B 1 : 10**

1 Aluminium/glass façade
2 Joint, elastic on the outside
3 Mineral wool lining
4 Joint, elastic on the inside
5 40 × 95 mm still plate
6 Façade anchoring
7 Concrete element
8 IPE 180
9 45 × 195 mm wooden beam
10 225 mm mineral wool
11 45 × 195 mm wooden beam
12 Vapour seal
13 30 mm lath for plasterwork
14 2 × 13 mm plasterboard
15 19 mm planking
16 Roofing felt
17 Zinc capping
18 50 mm rigid foam insulating board
19 Interior wall lining (wood)
20 Sound-insulating wool
21 30 mm mineral wool
22 28 × 135 mm flooring sleepers

**All the interior walls are executed as flexible plasterboard framed-partition walls.**

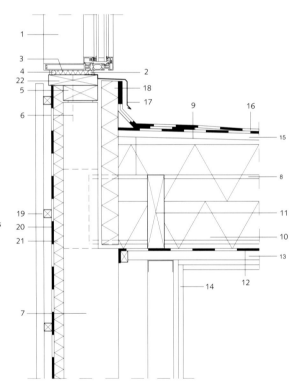

**Detail C 1 : 10**

The primary structure is composed of an inexpensive steel frame. The concrete, which gives a solid appearance, combines concrete and LECA façade elements.

**Building data**

| | |
|---|---|
| Property | Law court in Tarnby |
| Location | Blakklokkevej 4, Tarnby, Denmark |
| Client | Danish Ministry of Justice |
| Completion | 1997–2000 |
| Specialists | Teytaud, consultant engineer |
| | Svend Kierkegaard, landscape architect |
| Structure | Steel skeleton structure; façade: partly of aluminium and glass, partly of LECA elements with stucco facing |

# Office Block in Fellbach, Germany

Architects: Dollmann + Partner, Stuttgart

**Largely prefabricated and superbly spacious: this office building in Fellbach, Germany, is proof that a tight budget and successful architecture need not necessarily be mutually exclusive.**

Office blocks are as unsuitable for architectural experiments as residential buildings. Leaving aside the façade ornamentation – always a controversial issue – entrances calculated to convey prestige, conference areas and boardrooms, even those high-rise buildings that impress by their immensity are usually little more than office cells stacked on top of one another, often complete with a chicken-battery atmosphere. And back in the 19th century, Friedrich Nietzsche noted that the most prominent feature of modern office buildings is their sheer size. Although in recent years they have become the focus of research on ecological service installations, the real aim is, as often as not, cost cutting. Like factory floors, office buildings are subject to the functional and profit-seeking ambitions of the clients commissioning their construction. Exceptions to the "off-the-peg" approach so widespread in town and city centres and industrial estates are becoming increasingly rare. And those that do exist are mainly to be found in companies of the "new middle class", which are caught in the clutches of both politicians and venture capitalists.

For Stuttgart architect Frank Dollmann, the profitability criteria of his client, imt Nagler, a service company that develops and implements automation plans for industrial undertakings, formed the basis of a solution that is not only a convincing innovative variation on the theme of a house-within-a-house, but above all a fascinating spatial entity extending over four stories. The precisely cut, compact cube has grey-painted east and west façades composed of standalone slag concrete elements. On the south and north

sides, the building opens up onto the countryside through a glass façade borne by wooden elements. Three more open floors, organised according to the same system, rise above the square-shaped ground floor. The upper floors, supported by a steel skeleton, are turned 90 degrees around the central axis. A void 14.5 m high, 20 m long and 5 m wide links the individual workplaces, which are distributed across the floors, allowing visual contact over several stories.

Staff performing noisy operations, as well as the conference, recreation and sanitary rooms are all accommodated in containers (with interior veneer/panelling) slotted into the tubular steel frame, one to each floor. The individual atmosphere of each workplace is ensured by its unique positioning in relation to the glass façade, since the lighting and room heights are different in different parts of the building. That this atmosphere is also accepted by the staff is demonstrated by the absence of potted plants and other similarly tried-and-tested measures – which are usually a failure from the aesthetic point of view – generally employed in even the most progressive administration buildings to give office cells an individual feel. Access to the workplaces is via a lift tower sheathed in fair-face concrete and light steel, as well as by light-steel stairs that turn at each floor.

All materials have been left untreated and very few of the component parts are clad. The walkways, staircases and railings, the open service ducts and composite steel floors, the tubular steel frame filled with concrete up to the third floor to serve as a firewall) create a shimmering picture that offers a surprising contrast to the

The slag concrete façade of the compact cube is grey on the east and the west sides.

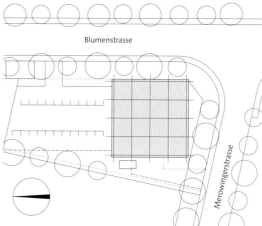

Blumenstrasse

Merowingerstrasse

Site plan 1:1,000

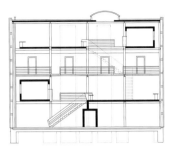

Cross section 1:1,000

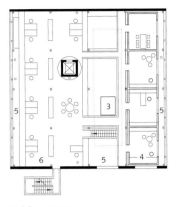

3rd floor 1:500

1 Demonstration and
  entrance area
2 Assembly area
3 Rack
4 Container
5 Air space
6 Bonding area

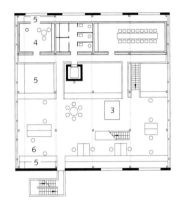

2nd floor 1:500

The façades facing
north and south
are made of glass
borne by wooden
elements.

1st floor 1:500

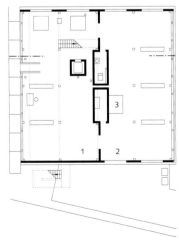

Ground floor 1:500

severe, accentuated order and discipline of the external form (the two glass facades notwithstanding). At the same time, all these elements complement the external form to create a whole that generously favours individuality. Yet nowhere does the building give cause to doubt – nor indeed is this the intention of its conspicuous purism – that it is a place of work. Although the somewhat opaque service provided by the client is not directly expressed in the building's design, it is conveyed in an impression that awakens interest. It is a pietistic Swabian style, and a very pleasant variation on the theme of "less is more": it is not the finished work with all its embellishments and gesturing that is supposed to speak to us, but simply work in a pleasant atmosphere.

The brief was hardly evocative of an "architecture parlante". The only stipulations were the small budget, the completion date and a utilisable space of roughly 1,200 m². There was no location, no site and no room programme. The architect's solution was to rely extensively on prefabricated elements and the – visible – autarky of the building elements, while carefully considering the users' mode of work - which is not so different from that of an architect's office. Implementation was largely a matter of assembly rather than bricklaying (apart from the trapezoidal plate floors and the assembly area on the ground floor), along with the deployment of economical furnishings and multi-use open spaces.

It goes without saying that the tight budget also applies to the running costs: hence, the building is not only lit and ventilated naturally, but also cooled naturally, using the differences in temperature between day and night. Finally, the stack effect is also exploited whenever conditions permit. The building, which has so far received only moderate recognition in the form of the Auszeichnung guter Bauten (Good Buildings Award) of the Baden-Württemberg branch of the Association of German Architects, is a masterly and, in part, exemplary contribution to the architecture of office buildings. And even if its architecture is not really generalisable – owing to the lack of references to its urban surroundings – certain aspects merit further development.

All materials – wood, veneer, glass, pumice concrete, in situ concrete and galvanised steel – are untreated. Hardly any of the building elements are clad.

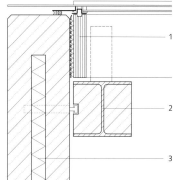

1 Wood and aluminium façade with stepped glazing
2 HEA 220 column with concrete (composite column)
3 Slag-concrete element wall with core insulation
4 Weather-resistant and antiglare hood, hot-dip galvanized sheet steel
5 Lamella windows with thermally separate profiles

Corner of building 1:15

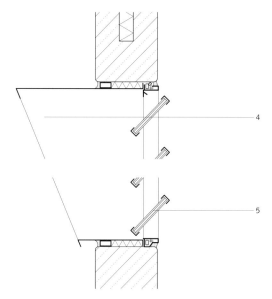

Ventilation element 1:15

1 Continuous row light elements, three-layer transparent acrylic glass as ventilation flap and smoke and heat extractor system
2 Hot-dip galvanized sheet-metal frame
3 Installation fixture in sheet-steel ceiling
4 Core bore holes for supply lines
5 Heating pipes
6 Cable lines

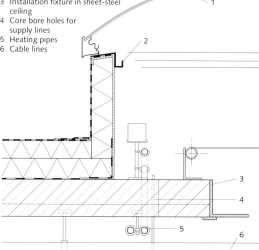

Continuous row lights 1:15

The building receives natural lighting and ventilation. It is also cooled naturally, using the temperature differences between day and night.

**Building data**

| | |
|---|---|
| Property | Office building |
| Location | Blumenstrasse 47, 70736 Fellbach, Germany |
| Client | Inke Nagler, represented by imt Nagler GmbH |
| Completion | 1998 |
| Specialists | Heinz Kipp, structural design |
| Structure | Prefabricated steel skeleton, skimmed reinforced concrete holorib ceilings prefabricated container integrated into steel skeleton |
| Materials | Wood, veneer laminated wood, glass, slag concrete, in situ concrete, galvanised zinc (all untreated) |
| Size of plot | 1,640 m² |
| Gross floor area | 1,805 m² |
| Volume | 6,414 m³ |
| Construction cost | € 1,300/m² |

# The Administration and Warehouse Building in Bad König, Germany

Architects: Beckenhaub + Hohm, Bad König

Supermarkets standing alongside high-rise buildings, residential buildings nestling up against halls of aerated concrete – a confusing combination of gable, mono-pitch and compass roofs: this is the environment, characterised by an almost destructive diversity, that was selected for the new administration and warehouse building in Bad König. Is it possible to do anything right at a place where so much has gone wrong?

It most certainly is, as the design by architects Beckenhaub + Hohm demonstrates, for it is straightforward without being monotonous, timeless rather than fashionable. These qualities ensure that the new building stands out in an otherwise jumbled environment.

The building has two sections: storage and administration. And a glance along the façade identifies them: the warehouse part is enclosed in an elongated reinforced concrete slab inserted forcefully into the gently inclined site. This monolith only opens towards the forest and meadows in the west, whilst the cantilevered roof, supported by taut cables, accentuates the orthogonal alignment of the whole. The glazed administration section looks as if it has been pushed onto this massive base from the street side. Shear walls and openings are placed at regular intervals, a strict symmetry that receives further emphasis in the entrance area: here the two central shear walls open out to the reception area, where a ramp leads up into the building. The pillars conceal an open atrium where the few visible materials are brought face to face: concrete, glass and clinker.

This is a building that retreats before the eye. And this is precisely what lends the design its special quality. All attention is focused on the form and the material: the Bockorner clinker in a mixture of grey and red, the storey-high windows, the smooth, calm surface of the fair-face concrete. The double-leaf sandwich elements of highly compressed watertight concrete do not seek to conceal their functional character, quite the opposite: structuring elements and economy were the theme underlying this design, in which open cross joints lend the surface form. The large concrete panels serve as a basic module determining the distribution and size of the concrete pillars. No attempt is made to hide the fact that the peat clinker is mere facing, and the reinforced concrete structure is also visible in front of the well set back windows. The façade dynamics are accentuated by the aluminium-slat sunshades, which, when closed, recall the corrugated iron facades of the surrounding industrial halls. This rather ironic allusion demonstrates that good architecture can succeed with simple means.

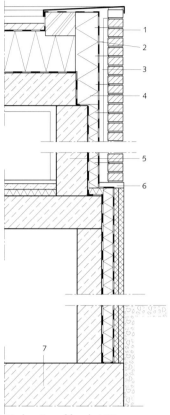

**Vertical section of façade 1:50**

1 Faced brickwork
2 Parapet cladding anchor
3 Air space
4 Fibrous glass mat
5 Reinforced concrete load-bearing shell
6 Sill
7 Reinforced concrete slab

**Articulation: The concrete slabs serve as modules determining the distribution and scale of the glass and bricked surfaces.**

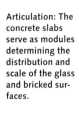

# The Steinweg Housing Development in Regensburg, Germany

Architects: Fink + Jocher, Munich

**Top-quality housing and inexpensive construction need not be mutually exclusive, as the Munich architects Fink + Jocher have again impressively demonstrated in the Steinweg Housing Development in Regensburg.**

With unusual plans, a prefabricated series-produced construction system and innovative standards, the architects pulled out all the stops to cut costs. Furthermore, the Steinweg Housing Development could not be better situated: it is surrounded by a wildly romantic biotope with an earthy, forest smell; peaceful and idyllic, but very close to the centre of Regensburg. In 1995 the client, the Regensburg construction company Dorrer SF Bau, invited architects to participate in a design competition for the vacated site of a former brickworks. The brief required a mixture of very diverse dwellings. Munich architects Fink + Jocher won the competition with their compact development concept, which (excluding the space occupied by the biotope) envisaged a floor space index of 1.1. The first phase of construction involved the construction of 35 dwellings in the northern part of the site. These radiant white houses, which were completed in 1997, formed a neighbourhood of their own.

### A Social Mix and Spirited Diversity

The second and third construction phases were completed in early 2000. The striking colour scheme, based on a warm reddish-orange hue, provided an enchanting contrast with the buildings already finished. In these final phases, 100 dwellings were constructed, of which approximately half were state subsidised, the others being financed privately. The broad spectrum of dwelling types – ranging from small two-room flats to flats for disabled people to spacious maisonettes and three-storey terraced houses – was aimed at a rich mix of residents with a wide variety of needs and desires, and whose very diversity and proximity to one another were intended to infuse life into the settlement.

However, as Thomas Jocher points out, the concept of a social mix only functions when the various groups are allowed to establish their own boundaries. In the Steinweg settlement, this requirement is addressed by means of the main access road running through the middle of the development: the state-subsidised homes are located on the eastern side of the road, whilst the privately financed terraced houses and flats are on its west. The three-storey buildings have been arranged perpendicularly to the eastern slope to integrate the surrounding green areas into the settlement. Beneath the development on the west side, a parking level serving both sides of the settlement has been created which pushes into the slope, so that the entrances and open spaces of the three-storey terraced houses are situated a level above that of the street. The dominant four-storey buildings facing the street have been constructed on pillars and contain large two and four-room flats.

### Inexpensive Housing Projects

The eastern section of the settlement, the five buildings in the social housing scheme, form part of the Bavarian Land government's pilot scheme for "inexpensive housing projects". The aim here, within the framework of a competition, was to demonstrate approaches that used different building materials and structural systems in such a way as to cut costs. In the process, standards were to be presented for debate.

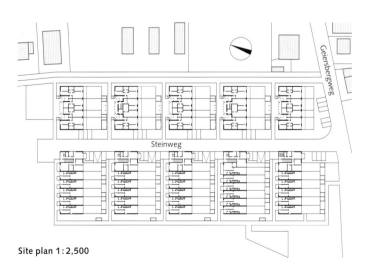

Site plan 1:2,500

The unusual constellation of partners involved in the construction project created ideal conditions for cutting costs. The client not only runs a reinforced-concrete works, but also owns the company that executed the project. On the one hand, this restricted experimentation to developing the structural system of precast reinforced concrete units. On the other, a rare opportunity thereby arose to optimise the system by encouraging close collaboration between the architect and those executing the work. This had an extremely favourable impact on costs: system-immanent parameters, which play an important role in series production, transport and the assembly of prefabricated units in situ, formed an integral part of the planning from the very start and influenced the final design. For example, the short span (3.4 m) of the ceiling elements and the arrangement of the apertures in the outside-wall sections were specifically optimised for the manufacturing and transport process.

### The Enormous Cost-Cutting Potential was Fully Exploited

Another way Fink + Jocher managed to lower costs was by dispensing with some floor elements generally prescribed by German standards. They economised on screed and footstep-sound insulation, covering both sides of the precast floor elements instead with a soft, springy material: either carpeting or PVC with a soft underside. At the same time, the reinforced concrete ceiling was 20 cm thicker than normal and designed to provide insulation against footstep noise.

Other cost killers included the open stairwells, which also encourage communication, reducing basement areas to the prescribed minimum of 5 square metres per dwelling (and only two of the five houses have basements) and – last but not least – bundling all the service installations into a central service line in the bathroom. In order to reduce the length of the individual lines, the heating pipes run directly from the bathroom into the living rooms. This also explains the unusual plans: the single rooms are accessed decentrally via the living room and the kitchen. Consequently, the internal circulation routes and the service installations do not cross.

The overall result is impressive. Including the two dwellings with flush thresholds, and a common room for use by the residents in the southern house, the architects succeeded in reducing costs to 830 euros per square metre. This figure is about 250 euros less than the permissible upper limit of 1,073 euros stipulated for subsidised dwellings. In this way, Fink + Jocher have again impressively demonstrated that top-quality dwellings and low-cost house construction are not mutually exclusive. And this achievement has also been recognised by a number of competition juries: from the Wüstenrot Stiftung's design prize to the Putz prize for architecture.

To top it all, residents in this settlement are also guaranteed free sunshine. And all the architects did this was to playfully use the hue saturation values required by thermal insulation systems to reduce "surface tension" caused by solar impact. Changes in colour at the edges – luminous orange on the south and west façades, and rich deep brick red on the north and east sides – create the impression of light and shadow. Even on cloudy days the sun seems to be shining.

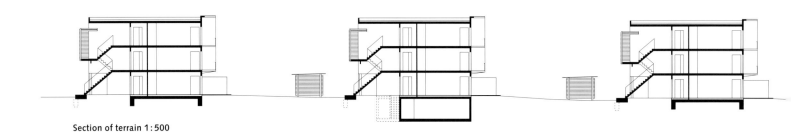

Section of terrain 1 : 500

The building's primary structure is composed almost exclusively of surface-finished prefabricated reinforced concrete elements produced in the client's precasting factory. This process considerably reduced construction time and costs.

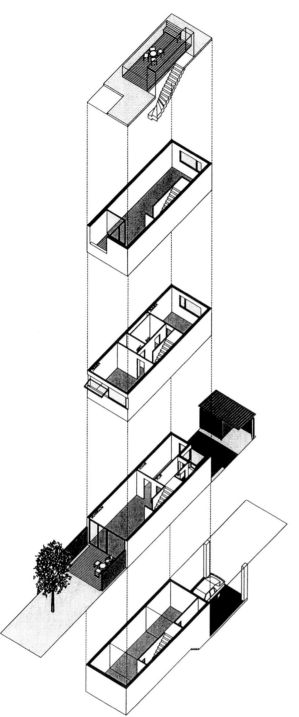

Illustration of component elements

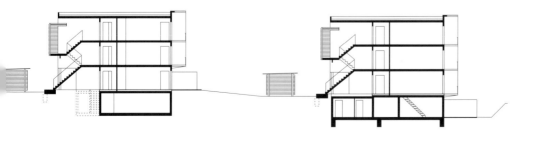

1 Stairs
  ratio of rise and tread
2 Prefabricated elements
  both sides surface finished
3 Wooden beams
  optimised material properties
4 Basements as required
5 Series production
6 Switch room
7 Open plan
8 Stairwell
  with an economically executed
  façade
9 Installation
  short lines
10 Short width
  max. 3.4 m

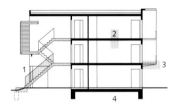

Section AA 1:500

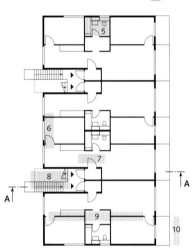

1st floor 1:500
Ground plan concept

1 Roof structure:
  substratum 50 mm
  mat filter
  drain layer 50 mm
  separating layer (anti-trickle)
  thermal insulation 120 mm
2 External wall structure:
  prefabricated reinforced concrete
  element
  thermal insulation panels 90 mm
  plaster
3 Galvanised flat-steel railing
4 Wooden beam, BSH spruce
5 Floor structure:
  carpet/PVC
  footstep-sound insulation
  precast reinforced concrete element
  200 mm
6 Floor structure
  carpet/PVC
  footstep-sound insulation
  polyethylene sheeting
  footstep-sound insulation 15 mm
  thermal insulation 50 mm
  reinforced concrete element 250 mm
7 Lath floor, larch

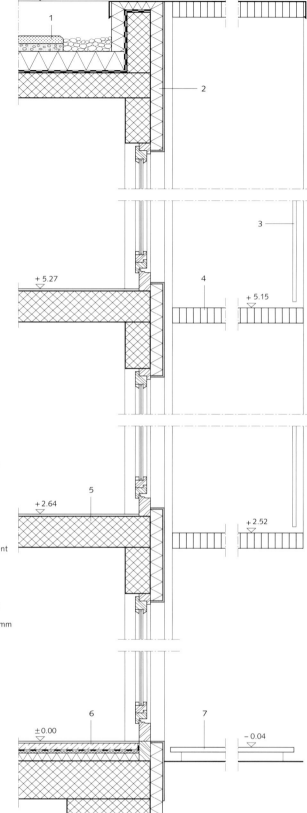

Vertical section of façade 1:25

Load-bearing exterior and interior walls consisting of 14 cm non-bearing interior walls of 10 cm-thick prefabricated reinforced-concrete elements. The prefabricated walls and ceilings of the terraced houses are 26 cm and 20 cm thick respectively. All of the stairs, the parking level and all of the non-insulated surfaces (walls dividing gardens) are of fair-face concrete.

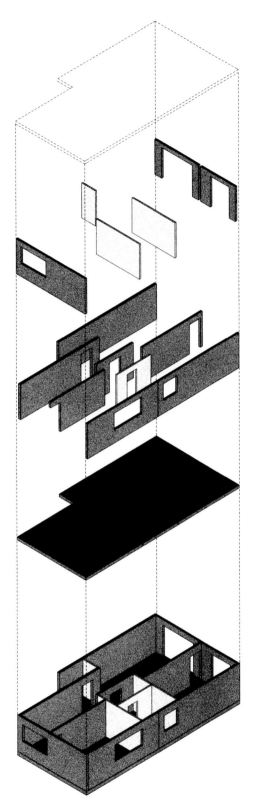

Illustration of component elements

**Building data**

| | |
|---|---|
| Property | Steinweg Housing Development |
| Location | Arnulf-Enders-Strasse 1-61, 93059 Regensburg, Germany |
| Client | Dorrer SF Bau GmbH, Regensburg |
| Specialists | Weidmüller, landscape architect, Regensburg Stockgruber, landscape architect, Buch/Erlbach |
| Structure | Prefabricated element / precast reinforced concrete elements |
| Materials | Simple untreated materials, fair-face concrete, solid wood, laminated wood |
| Size of plot | 25,385 m² |
| Construction costs | € 831/m² |

# The Sophie Scholl School in Giessen, Germany

Architects: Heinrich and Peter Diehl, Giessen

**A heterogeneous reference to the world outside, an almost solemn atmosphere within: for this pilot school for both disabled and "normal" children, the architects have created a pleasantly understated yet clearly defined building.**

"A classroom designed in the new style is hardly separate from the outside world. Being taught in such a school is like being taught out in the open air, only here one has the added advantage of having a boundary, so necessary for concentration, around the room." – Thus wrote Fritz Wichert in 1928 in an article published by Ernst May in the magazine Das Neue Frankfurt. The ideas developed by Wichert, then director of the Frankfurter Kunstschule, and others were put into practice during May's era by other agencies. That same year, the Frankfurt municipal building department reached an agreement with the education authority to teach henceforth only in the so-called pavilion system. Their argument (which could have come from Wichert) was based on a desire to "take into consideration the need for lessons outdoors: in touch with nature, with fresh air, the light and the sun".

The Sophie Scholl School in Giessen (about 65 km from Frankfurt am Main) is more than a contemporary attempt to implement propositions and typologies that are beginning to show their age. Even so, looking at the building on the eastern outskirts of the city, one cannot avoid thinking of the "May era", with all its pathos. Wide sliding-doors abolish all opposition between the inside and outside worlds, extended horizontal windows cut into the façade, present a view of the carefully laid-out school garden. And even in the upper storey, the bordering forest is within physical reach thanks to the skylights and the low parapets. Hence, it is "like being taught out in the open air". And one day, as the ageing process already suggests, when the larch shuttering

finally assumes a greyish-silver hue, the building will simply disappear amongst the trees. The new architecture, says Wichert: "wants to establish contact with the ground, with the animals and plants; it teaches us a new kind of familiarity with the wind and the weather".

With this school, the client and sponsor, the association Lebenshilfe für geistig behinderte Menschen (counselling for mentally disabled people), has chosen a new path: disabled and "normal" children between the ages of six and twelve are taught at the Sophie Scholl School. Each class is supervised by three educators from 7.30 a.m. to 4.30 p.m. Furthermore, every classroom (60 m²) has direct access to an additional room half its size set aside for supervision. Whereas the classrooms face the garden (to the east and the south) the administration rooms, which follow the same 60:30 principle, are situated along the north side. The functional rooms, such as the gymnasium, two canteens, therapy rooms etc., are located on the west side. Their proportions also follow the same plan.

The building encloses a courtyard, which is surrounded by corridors running along the inside of the glazed walls bordering it. Unlike the wooden facing of the exterior fronts, the courtyard has a prestigious, almost solemn character: stern, rational, rather cool, and certainly not at all evocative of children. This impression is conveyed not only by the precise jointing of the floor slabs and the concrete columns holding the spherical lamps, but also, more than anything else, by the two-storey perystile-like porch above the entrance. In the two-storey entrance

**Site plan 1 : 2,500**

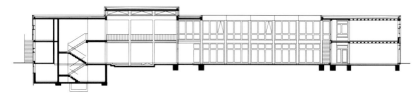

Section AA 1:750

hall, however, with its natural-stone floor and its effectively illuminated pillars and waffle ceiling, the stern, solemn atmosphere is sustained. The waffle ceiling is repeated in the classrooms. There, however, the concrete is deliberately given a sharp-edged appearance, an impression intensified by the lightweight formwork elements, the sealed joints and the precisely fitted hardboard panels. The fair-face concrete in the entrance halls and corridors is glazed; in the classrooms it has been sprayed with white emulsion.

In the approach taken by Peter Diehl, the school's architect, one might discern a certain affinity to Oswald M. Ungers' design principles. Indeed, Ungers' Frankfurt office was run by Diehl in the early 1980s. However, one can also detect similarities with Wichert here: the new architecture "seeks to use the design elements of line, area, corporeality (SPACE) and colour in the simplest manner possible and with the utmost clarity… It only uses that which is necessary, consciously moderating its means of expression, even to the point of austerity". The architect has consciously given the pilot school, whose disabled pupils normally tend to be marginalised by society, a clearly defined, rational, modest building. His is not an exalted design that would push the school – already fighting for economic survival – even closer to the brink. Diehl has given the children space to shape their own surroundings. And as sober as his design may appear, it is precisely its stern character that gives it the strength to brave and even foster expressions of the children's love of movement and joy in design. Or, as Wichert says: "What the mind shapes, shapes the mind".

The concrete on the exterior is untreated; only the horizontal planes of the aligned columns have been water-proofed.

All concrete shuttering systems use triangular batons. In order to execute this project the systems here had to be partly reconstructed. In other words, the supports and shuttering had to fit exactly and the joints be sealed to prevent the concrete water from leaking.

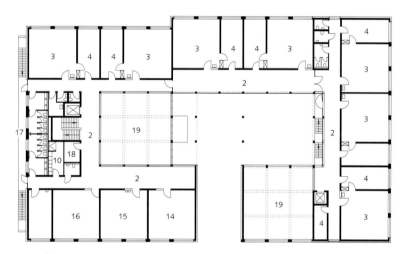

**Upper floor 1:750**

1 Assembly hall
2 Corridor
3 Classroom
4 Teaching material
5 Head teacher
6 Teachers
7 Administration
8 Dining area
9 Kitchen
10 Dish washing
11 Kiosk
12 Gymnasium
13 Equipment
14 Socialeducation
15 Art room
16 Therapy
17 Emergency escape balcony
18 Store-room
19 Air space

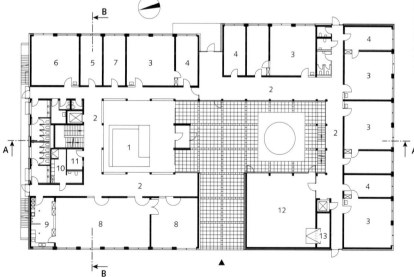

**Ground floor 1:750**

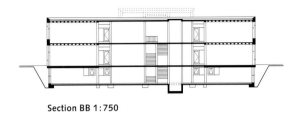

Section BB 1:750

The outer shell was executed
as a punctuated façade with
wooden windows. Larch
weatherboarding formwork is
mounted on the façade.

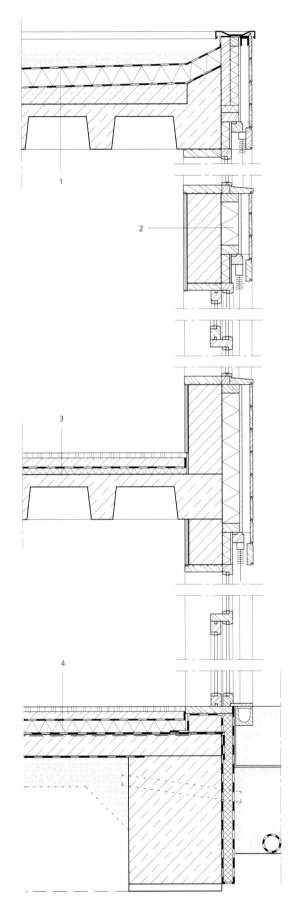

1   Roof structure
    5 cm coarse gravel 16/32
    roof skin
    12 cm heat insulating layer
    vapour proofing
    3-14 cm sloping screed
    30 cm ribbed ceiling of fair-face concrete

2   Wall structure
    2 cm shuttering, horizontal
    6 cm air space
    1 cm fibreboard
    12 cm insulation
    24 cm masonry
    1.5 cm interior plastering

3   Ceiling structure
    3 cm industrial parquet
    5 cm floating screed
    5 cm footstep-sound/thermal insulation
    30 cm ribbed ceiling of fair-face concrete

4   Floor structure
    3 cm industrial parquet
    5 cm floating screed
    19 cm thermal insulation
    horizontal impervious course
    first coating
    15 cm floor plate
    20 cm filter gravel

Vertical section 1:25

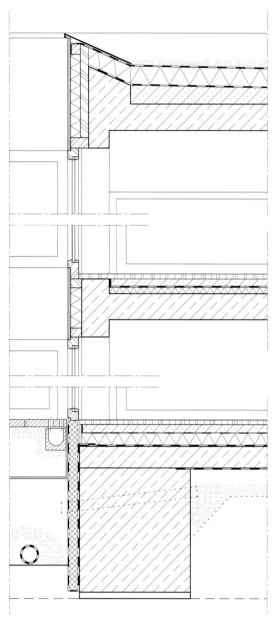

Roof structure
5.0 cm coarse gravel
roof skin
12.0 cm heat insulating layer
vapour proofing
first coating
3-14 cm sloping screed
18 cm fair-face concrete

Vertical section of courtyard façade 1:25

**Building data**

| | |
|---|---|
| **Building** | Sophie-Scholl-Schule |
| **Location** | Grünberger Strasse 224, 35394 Giessen, Germany |
| **Client** | Lebenshilfe Kreisvereinigung Giessen E.V. |
| **Specialists** | Neuhaus+Partner, Ing. Büro Weis service installations, Giessen, Ing. Büro Zettl, structural engineering, Giessen, Weis Ingenieurbüro VDI, electrical engineering, Mergeskirchen |
| **Structure** | Masonry, reinforced concrete |
| **Materials** | Simple untreated materials, fair-face concrete, solid wood, laminated wood |
| **Size of plot** | 24,611 m² / 7,376.12 m² |
| **Floor area** | 3,170 m² |
| **Construction cost** | € 1966/m² |

# Church in Valdemaqueda near Madrid, Spain

Architect: José Ignacio Linazasoro Rodríguez

**Not far from Madrid there stand the remains of a village church. Once almost completely destroyed, they have now been pieced together to form a unified whole. Here, structural fair-face concrete has been used in such a way that it is not at all recognisable as concrete.**

The houses in the small village of Valdemaqueda seem to have been scattered around at random. The parish, which has 470 inhabitants at most, is located about 70 kilometres from Madrid in an almost virgin mountain region. A rather modest Late Gothic church formerly stood here. After it had been almost totally destroyed during the 1940s, all that remained standing were parts of the apse and a Renaissance door.

José Ignazio Linazasoro Rodríguez, a Madrid architect, was commissioned to "resurrect" the building. After completing his doctoral thesis in 1981, Linazasoro, who was born in San Sebastián in 1947, was offered a teaching post at the department of architecture at the University of Vallodolid, where he taught from 1983 to 1988. In 1988 he moved to Madrid. It was with projects like the reconstruction of the church in Medina de Rioseco that he made a name for himself as a historian and restorer.

### Concrete and Gothic?

Linazasoro's strategy is to reconstruct buildings with modern means, approaching old structures with a contemporary concept. In the process, the architect's work is supposed to serve the concept, and not vice versa. Linazasoro applied this principle in the reconstruction of the church in Valdemaqueda. He added a cubic structure – a modern nave – to the ruins of the apse of the old stone church, with its mighty pier buttresses. A reinforced concrete wall, executed as a multi-shell reinforced concrete structure, forms the load-bearing core. The inner and outer shells are composed of brick masonry.

The façade has been faced with thin, light granite. At the interface between the old and new structures, a quadratic superstructure rises perpendicular to the longitudinal axis of the building, taking up the entire width of the nave. Although, this structure resembles a fire station from afar, a small cross fixed to its outer edge identifies it as a church tower. The church's continuous overhead strip windows illuminate the interior with daylight.

### Striving for Simplicity and Playing with Light

An old Renaissance stone gateway arch with a triangular gable placed next to a corner on the southern front of the new building, with its smooth façade, conspicuously marks the entrance to this house of worship. As an *objet trouvé* visibly standing out from the building line, it frames the large, two-storey wooden church door. The door's two leaves have been given quite unusual treatment, "fitting together" above normal entrance height like two parts of a puzzle. To the left of the entrance, light enters the interior at about waist height through a small quadratic aperture. This, the only opening in the west wall, provides a dramatic setting for the stoup, which is carved into a quadratic, dark-grey granite block and projects from the wall. An open system of binders and joists arranged transversely to the north-south axis creates a low ceiling at this part of the nave. The fair-face/concrete spandrel beam is supported by a quadratic concrete pier. The end support bordering the tower is quite striking: a fair-face/concrete crossbeam stretching between the south and north walls establishes

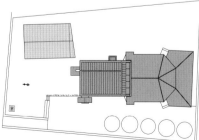

**Site plan 1 : 1,000**

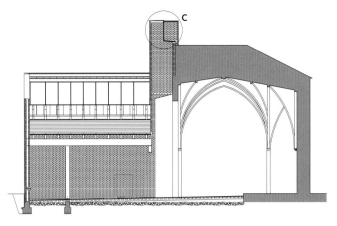

Longitudinal section 1 : 333 ¹/₃

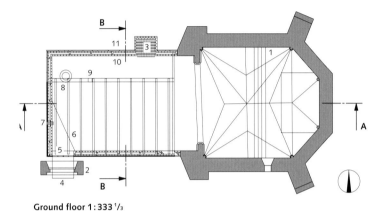

Ground floor 1 : 333 ¹/₃

1  Existing altar
2  Existing entrance portal
3  Confessional
4  Metal gate
5  Granite slab
6  Floor: polished concrete
7  Stoup
8  Font
9  Rafters
10  Double wall, brick masonry
11  Granite facing

**Building data**

| | |
|---|---|
| Building | Church of Valdemaqueda |
| Location | Valdemaqueda, Madrid, Spain |
| Client | The Parish of Valdemaqueda |
| Completion | 2001 |
| Specialist | Juan Carlos Corona Ruiz, engineering, Madrid |
| Materials | Reinforced concrete, granite, brick |
| Size of plot | 864 m² |
| Floor area | 285 m² |
| Construction cost | € 288,486/m² |

The two door leaves have been given quite unusual treatment, being "interlinked" above the actual entrance like a puzzle.

A reinforced concrete wall forms the load-bearing core. The inner and outer shell is of brick masonry.

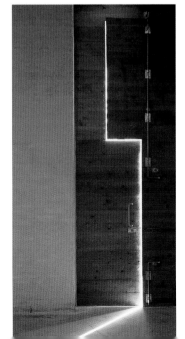

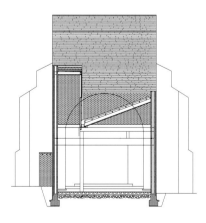

Cross section 1 : 333 ¹/₃

a clear dividing line across the room without obstructing the view. Only a beam-width higher begins the downstand beam of the rising tower wall. The concrete surfaces stand out against the simplicity of the grey-limewashed interior walls due to the irregular patterning of the saw-edges made by the horizontal, thin wooden shuttering boards. Another exceptional feature is the construction of the confessional, planned as an allusion to the pier buttresses of the Gothic sections of the church. The confessional's cubic form projects from the north wall of the nave. From inside the church, the confessional appears as a wide opening, with a raised landing, in the north wall.

For all the barrenness of its fittings and furnishings, the church interior, whose floor forms a long diagonal reaching as far as the chancel, is enlivened by the unique atmosphere created by the light entering through the few apertures in the side walls and the two (transverse and longitudinal) overhead strip windows. Light designers are well aware of the positive impact of grey-concrete surfaces, particularly in buildings situated in a Mediterranean environment. And Linazasoro also knows how to exploit this effect to illuminate his church interior. He consciously employs light to mark out the spatial centre of the church: the brightness radiating from the strip windows high up in the tower contrasts with the gloominess of the apse below, with its old ribbed vault. There, in the semi-darkness, one can barely make out the contours of a small Renaissance altar. At the front of the new nave, another strip window extends across the entire length of the north side in the turret. There, it not only creates an interesting spatial counter-pole to the low wooden-joist ceiling, but – by allowing thin fingers of light to enter – also lends the illumination of the side wall a mystical quality.

The façade was faced with thin light-coloured granite tiles.

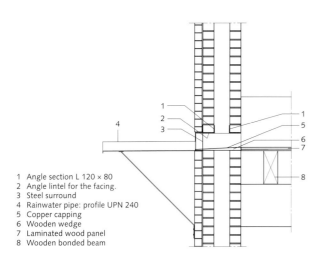

1 Angle section L 120 × 80
2 Angle lintel for the facing.
3 Steel surround
4 Rainwater pipe: profile UPN 240
5 Copper capping
6 Wooden wedge
7 Laminated wood panel
8 Wooden bonded beam

Detail of gargoyle 1:40

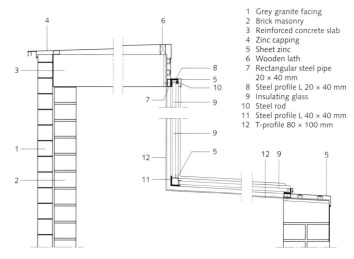

1 Grey granite facing
2 Brick masonry
3 Reinforced concrete slab
4 Zinc capping
5 Sheet zinc
6 Wooden lath
7 Rectangular steel pipe 20 × 40 mm
8 Steel profile L 20 × 40 mm
9 Insulating glass
10 Steel rod
11 Steel profile L 40 × 40 mm
12 T-profile 80 × 100 mm

Detail A 1:20

# The Protestant Church Centre in Hanover, Germany

Architect: Prof. Dipl. Ing. Bernhard Hirche, Hamburg

**Where the wind once left its trail in the cornfields, streets now lend structure to the most modern of housing developments. Everything is novel at the EXPO settlement, which represents an attempt to integrate a rich variety of dwellings into a church centre.**

The residents of the Kronberg Settlement are called upon to live with one another in a manner that is both ecologically and economically sound. This settlement at the southeast of Hanover was conceived as an EXPO exhibit, as an exemplary form of dwelling for the 21st century. In the long term, 140 hectares are to be developed with the construction of low-energy houses and a large share of state-subsidised homes.

The focal point is a square that almost seems as if it weren't there. Commercial buildings and a large vacant building site occupy one side. Opposite stand a chemist superstore, an Italian restaurant, a socio-cultural neighbourhood centre and the Protestant church centre. The church, the parish and vicar's house, two residential buildings with 6 owner-occupied flats and 15 state-subsidised flats (three of which are furnished to accommodate the handicapped) are enclosed by a fair-face concrete frame the height of a building. The complex forms a distinct unit set apart from its urban context, and offers a home, in the immediate vicinity of the church, to single parents, the formerly homeless and senior citizens.

## A Modern Cloister

The Hamburg architect, Professor B. Hirche, assembled the church-centre buildings after the fashion of a classical cloister so that they constitute a rectangular settlement enclosing a courtyard. Thus grouped, the buildings create wide and narrow spaces – an artistically designed "Paradise", as it is called – in the courtyard. Fountains, water basins and a watercourse symbolise life. Shielded but not entirely cut off from

its urban surroundings, the terraced area, which is further structured by paths and stairways, provides space for both contemplation and community events. Fair-face and reinforced concrete elements (the materials of which the stair stringers, the retaining and courtyard walls surrounding the complex are made) and modest vegetation underline the sedate atmosphere of the whole. The gardens in front of the owner-occupied flats and the covered walks linking the subsidised flats help lend cohesion to social life inside the complex. A short path leads across the courtyard to the vicarage and the sexton's house, which are linked to the community house and the church by a "cloister". The cloister glazing makes the residential building's red, blue and yellow plaster façade glow in powerful pastel shades. The colourful design of this modern cloister accentuates the individuality of its residents and the diversity of facilities serving their needs.

## Monolithic – at First Sight

The diversity of life inside the complex reinforces the overriding design concept, which involved enclosing the premises with a wall the height of the buildings inside – a powerful gesture that infuses security into the entire complex. To implement this concept at low cost, the sections of the wall to which the "warm" building sections are attached on the interior were executed as exterior ventilated-cavity masonry walls clad with fibrated concrete panel. Since all signs of where the grey-dyed panel cladding was attached flush to the fair-face concrete sections have been well concealed, the complex initially strikes one

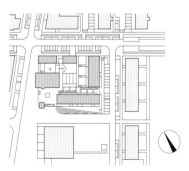

Site plan 1:4,000

as monolithic. Only on coming closer does one notice that the windows, the apertures, the wall openings, the grey fibrated concrete panels (which, like the joints in the fair-face concrete, accentuate the horizontals) and the fair-face concrete enclosing wall all serve to heighten the façade structure. Veneer plywood boards (Beto-planplatten) were used for the formwork on the fair-face concrete surfaces and the joints sealed with a plastic strip approx. 20cm wide and 2mm deep, structuring the concrete in the process. The strut holes have been sealed flush with the surface so that they will not detract from its appearance.

However, the complex is by no means a confined space (claustrum = cloister). Three-storey-high passages and small access paths passing over stairs and ramps lure visitors to the small forecourt in front of the church.

### A Concrete Apse

Giving emphasis to the projecting rectangular church by erecting a fair-face concrete wall in the western façade has also distinctly accentuated the feeling of space. The grill façade also gives the church a more striking appearance from the outside. The façade is mounted on three sides in front of the storey-high windows. In this way, it not only encloses the church interior, which lies on an east-west axis, but also slightly subdues the light entering the building. Under normal circumstances, there is enough room for about 180 people inside this amply illuminated rectangular building. Thanks to the variable seating, the hall can be rearranged to suit very different religious purposes. It can also be extended by the adjacent community rooms. The "apse" crowns the eastern end of the church. Its interior was executed in fair-face concrete, the exterior being composed of precast reinforced concrete elements. Narrow coloured windows, designed by Jochem Poensgen, create distinct accents in the smooth light-grey wall. The gallery, the ceiling and the downstand beams in the church are likewise made of in situ cast fair-face concrete, while the filigree floors have been topped with concrete. The light grey of the apse and ceiling contrasts with the black asphalt floor tiles and the black chairs. And one may be sure that many people would love to take a seat here – and not only the church-centre residents.

To implement the overriding design concept, which involved enclosing the premises with a wall the height of the buildings inside, at low cost, the sections of the wall to which the "warm" building sections are attached on the interior were executed as exterior ventilated-cavity masonry walls clad with fibrated concrete panels.

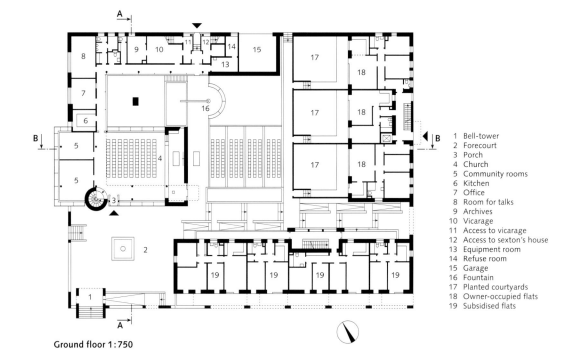

1 Bell-tower
2 Forecourt
3 Porch
4 Church
5 Community rooms
6 Kitchen
7 Office
8 Room for talks
9 Archives
10 Vicarage
11 Access to vicarage
12 Access to sexton's house
13 Equipment room
14 Refuse room
15 Garage
16 Fountain
17 Planted courtyards
18 Owner-occupied flats
19 Subsidised flats

Ground floor 1:750

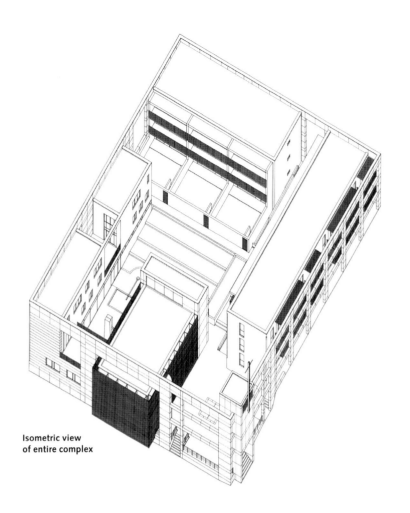

Isometric view
of entire complex

Upper left and right: the
thermal insulation panels on
buildings within the complex
are rendered in different colours to reinforce the impact
of the wall.
Right: a spiral staircase,
leading up to a gallery, is
concealed behind the blue
façade.

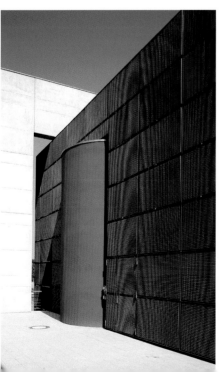

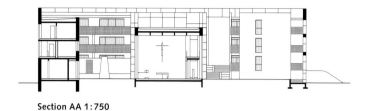

**Section AA 1:750**

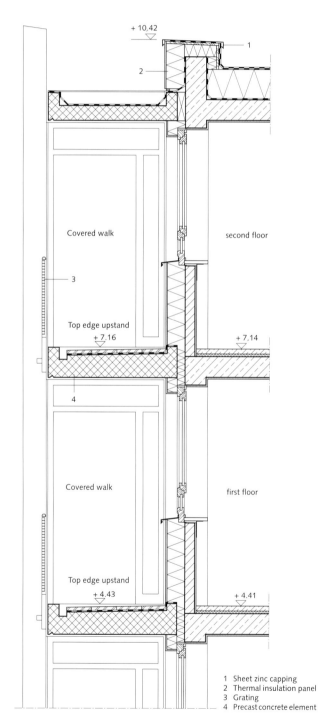

+ 10,42

1

2

Covered walk

second floor

3

Top edge upstand

+ 7,16

+ 7,14

4

Covered walk

first floor

Top edge upstand

+ 4,43

+ 4,41

1 Sheet zinc capping
2 Thermal insulation panel
3 Grating
4 Precast concrete element

**Vertical section of covered walk 1:40**

**Building data**

| | |
|---|---|
| Property | church centre with integrated subsidised and owner-occupied homes |
| Location | Kronsberg/Hanover |
| Client | Ev.-Luth. Stadtkirchenverband, Gesellschaft für Bauen und Wohnen Hannover mbH, Hanover |
| Completion | 2000 |
| Specialists | Dr. Ing. D. Hage & Partner, structural design, Braunschweig |
| Structure | Solid, reinforced concrete and masonry, precast concrete components, transom-and-mullion with grating curtain wall, fibrated-concrete-slab curtain wall and composite thermal insulating system |
| Materials | Steel, glass, in situ cast fair-face concrete, precast reinforced concrete elements |
| Size of plot | 3225.72 m² |
| Floor area | 4355 m² |
| Construction cost | € 918/m² |

The individual buildings, i.e. the church, the community room, the vicarage and the sexton's house with the roof terrace, the owner-occupied flats with their planted court-yards, and the subsidised flats opening onto a covered walkway, are all enclosed by a concrete wall with optimal-ly allocated entrances.

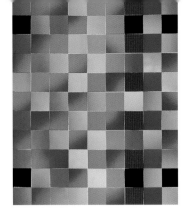

The church windows, designed by the artist Jochem Poensgen, set accents in the smooth light-grey wall.

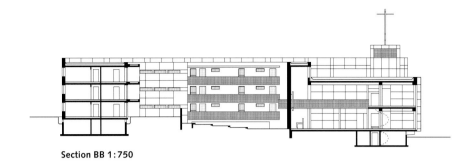

**Section BB 1:750**

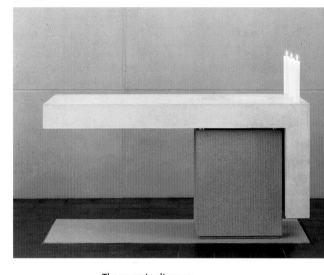

The concrete altar was designed by the architect.

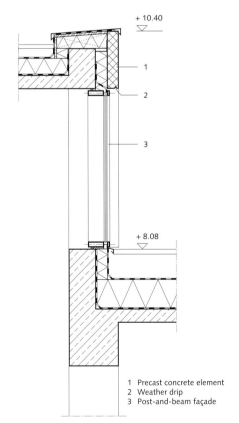

+ 10.40

1
2

3

+ 8.08

1  Precast concrete element
2  Weather drip
3  Post-and-beam façade

**Vertical section of church window 1:40**

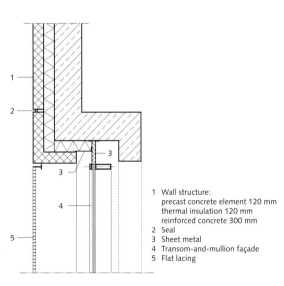

1

2

3
3

4

5

1  Wall structure:
   precast concrete element 120 mm
   thermal insulation 120 mm
   reinforced concrete 300 mm
2  Seal
3  Sheet metal
4  Transom-and-mullion façade
5  Flat lacing

**Vertical section of prefabricated façade of church 1:40**

# The Carmelite Convent in Wemding, Germany

Architect: Karl Frey, diocesan- and university architect, Eichstätt

**The Carmelite convent in Wemding looks as if it has been cast in one piece. Rough concrete faces the outside world, clear glass is dominant vis-à-vis the garden, and inside warm chestnut prevails.**

The Carmelite Order does not have to worry about new recruits – on the contrary. During the past few years, the flock of sisters has grown so rapidly that some nuns have had to move: out of the main residence in Speyer and off to the Palatinate. Thirteen of the women found a new home in Wemding, behind the thick walls of an old Capuchin monastery in a simple 17th-century church with an idyllic cloister garden and a peaceful hermitage. Unused for many years, the rooms obviously needed refurbishing. There was not enough space to accommodate visitors, let alone a dining-hall, an almonry, another for disabled people, work rooms with devotional articles, and three rooms for conversation.

### A New Carmel

It was time for a new Carmel. Inspired by diocese and university architect Karl Frey, the Order extended the church axis to create an almost quadratic building defining the access to the section of the cloister open to the public. Not having a base, the huge milky-white walls rise dramatically from the ground, forming a monolith of fairface concrete. Terraced in accordance with the sloping site, the stone colossus crouches respectfully before the sublime historical church. On the north side, the building presents a uniform front to the noisy street. On the south, the facades of the workshops on the ground floor and (a floor higher) the guestrooms with their large glass windows look out onto the greened courtyard. The terraced form of the building obviates the risk of intrusive gazing by visitors into the quadrangle.

As the nuns had very few specific requests, the historical cell structure of the Carmelite was retained when the old cloister was restored. All the sisters wanted was a table, a bed and a chair. Seven to eight square metres sufficed. In addition, there were two common washing-rooms, each with a bathtub, a shower and two washbasins. Frey was more generous in his treatment of the church interior: respecting the strict religious conception of the Carmelites, he redesigned two areas as distinct zones. An iron grille and sliding doors of chestnut separated the choir reserved for the nuns from the benches of the faithful. All the new installations maintain a respectful distance from the historical shell, in the church as well as in the cloister. Every effort has been made to show restraint in this regard.

### Materials

The richness of asceticism is also evident in the choice of materials: concrete, natural stone, wood, glass and steel. The almost seamless fair-face concrete walls, formed in a chipboard skin, have a rough and lively appearance. And the addition of Dyckerhoff White has given the two-layered external wall a rich creamy hue, harmonising with the surrounding countryside and the adjacent church. A milky white has also been used for the floors, which are covered with local Jurassic limestone, as well as for the church cloister, the cloister courtyard, and the area around the altar. Red chestnut offers a warm contrast to the hard stone. The furniture, the floors in the sisters' cells, the sliding wall in the newly designed altar, wythes concealing the modern service

The old and the new
define a semi-public
forecourt.

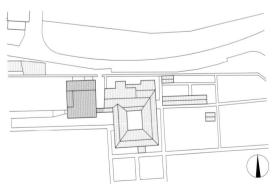

Site plan 1 : 2,500

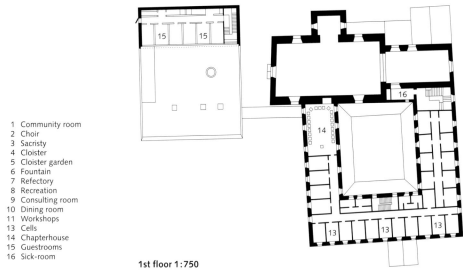

1 Community room
2 Choir
3 Sacristy
4 Cloister
5 Cloister garden
6 Fountain
7 Refectory
8 Recreation
9 Consulting room
10 Dining room
11 Workshops
13 Cells
14 Chapterhouse
15 Guestrooms
16 Sick-room

1st floor 1:750

The semicircular opening casts natural light into the dining room.

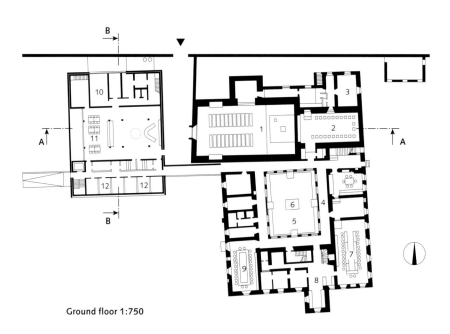

Ground floor 1:750

installations, and partition walls separating the single rooms from one another – all are made of this modest yet strong material, which provides the ideal contrast to the raw concrete shell.

## Concrete Made to Measure

Erecting the concrete components demanded precision work, and an architect was constantly present. Removing the formwork called for great sensitivity. To ensure that the ties were in perfect optical alignment (the principle anchorage points in the exterior wall shells alternate horizontally at 1.4 m and 1.1 m; vertically they are spaced at intervals of one metre) the masons first had to pour the exterior shell. Then, using normal concrete (C20/25) and single-side formwork, they poured the interior shell supporting the core insulation with struts (instead of continuous ties). To minimise the appearance of seams and create a lively concrete texture, the construction company used 2.50 m x 4 m large-panel formwork for the exterior wall. Craftsmen joined two sections of shuttering at a time and then bolted on the pre-oiled, permeable formwork (panels measuring

5 m x 2 m x 19 mm). They then filled the drill-holes and put plastic foam sealing tape between the panel joints. As the company that mixed and delivered the concrete was only about one kilometre away from the site the masons worked without a solvent, adding only a small quantity of plasticiser. Using crane buckets, they added the concrete in layers of 50 cm. In each concreting process, the concrete head was 4 m. Using an internal vibrator, the concrete was then compacted twice, allowing a 30-minute interval. After the formwork was removed, the walls were sealed for two days in a foil placed 10 cm from the walls. Finally, the fitters drilled the holes in the fibrated concrete for reinforcement bars before mortaring them with a mix of quartz sand and white cement. The finished surface was treated hydrophobically to produce a concrete that feels like hard velvet, and a building that seems to rise from the ground like a rock: a monolith that subordinates itself to the historical fabric, yet nevertheless stands alongside it by virtue of its own strength.

**Warm wood at the entrance greets people arriving.**

**The gatehouse with its workshops, guestrooms and dining room faces the garden only.**

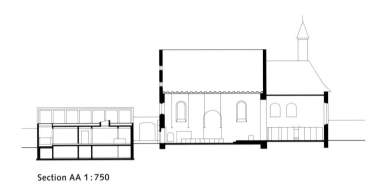

A glass corridor marks the transition to the modern age.

Section AA 1:750

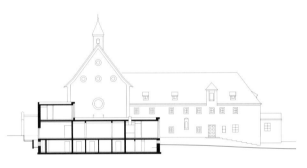

Section BB 1:750

The white fairface concrete façade recalls a cloister wall; only one aperture lets light into the guestrooms.

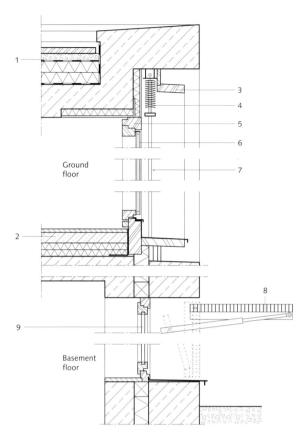

Ground floor

Basement floor

Vertical section of window front 1:25

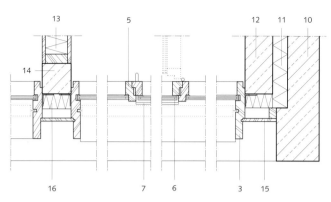

Horizontal section of window front

| | | |
|---|---|---|
| 1 | 280 mm | sheet roof with cladding of natural stone |
| 2 | 180 mm | floating concrete screed with oiled chestnut floor boards |
| 3 | 50 mm | solid oak frame, glazed |
| 4 | 70 mm | external blinds, aluminium |
| 5 | 135 mm | oak window frame, glazed |
| | 90 mm | oak window leaf, glazed |
| 6 | | mechanically mounted heat protection glass |
| 7 | 10 mm | safety rail of special steel round rod |
| 8 | | solar protection system of electrically operated swivelling aluminium sections |
| 9 | 68 mm | standard oak window varnished with heat protection glass |
| 10 | 220 mm | fair-face concrete, white |
| 11 | 110 mm | core insulation |
| 12 | 220 mm | fair-face concrete interior wall, grey |
| 13 | 250 mm | wooden dividing walls, chestnut surface, veneered and oiled |
| 14 | 250 mm | fair-face concrete pillar |
| 15 | 21 mm | solid oak board, varnished |
| 16 | 110 mm | insulation |

**Building data**

| | |
|---|---|
| Property | Carmelite Convent |
| Location | Kapuzinergraben 21, Wemding, Germany |
| Client | Diocese of Eichstätt |
| Completion | 2000 |
| Specialists | Sailer, Stephan und Partner, structural design, Munich |
| | Ingenieurbüro Walter Bamberger, electrical engineering, Pfünz |
| | Ingenieurbüro Koch Frey Donaubauer, service installations, Ingolstadt |
| | Landschaftsarchitekten Teuttsch Ritz Rebmann, landscaping, Munich |
| Structure | Solid construction in concrete, wood and steel |
| Materials | Steel, glass, concrete, prefabricated reinforced concrete elements |
| Size of plot | 17,751 m² |
| Floor area | 2,497.30 m² |
| Construction cost | Approx. € 2495/m² |

On the interior, fair-face concrete, natural stone, steel and wood satisfy the need for cloistral sternness.

# Judenplatz Museum in Vienna, Austria

Architects: Jabonegg & Pálffy, Vienna

**"Architecture one doesn't see", "invisible spaces", "architecture behind the façade"
– such are the terms architectural theorists generally use to describe the relatively
small oeuvre of Christian Jabornegg and Andras Pálffy.**

Whether it is a question of exhibition architecture for Dokumenta X, the exhibition rooms for the EA Generali Foundation, or conversion work on the Schoellerbank in the centre of Vienna, ostentatious architecture is simply not this duo's cup of tea. Their precise and disciplined contributions embody an oppositional stance not only to the transformation of Vienna into a collection of souvenirs, but also to the vanities of Austria's old stars, such as Coop Himmelblau, Hollein and Holzbauer.  They also resist the surface-minimalism – as fashionable as it is photogenic – of the recently much-touted "new office". Even so, as a commentator, one has to point out that the aforementioned bank conversion, for example, carried out by Dietmar Steinerhas, has been compared with Otto Wagner's famous Post Office Savings Bank. However, anyone who has ever visited the two architects in their rear-courtyard basement flat in District 4, Vienna, knows that even in Vienna  the world looks quite different seen from below.

And certainly no irony is intended in saying that with the project under review here Jabornegg & Pálffy found themselves on familiar terrain: behind the façade of the Mistrachihaus in a hidden corner of Judenplatz in Vienna – and below the ground too. Construction work on a memorial to the Austrian victims of the Shoa (for which Simon Wiesenthal suggested this site) uncovered the remains of a synagogue built around the mid-13th century and subsequently razed to the ground in the wake of a pogrom: the so-called Vienna Gesera of 1420-21. After work was interrupted, with the predictable heated

debates, a decision was finally taken to move the memorial designed by Rachel Whiteread a little and to establish a small museum – in the Misrachihaus – devoted to Jewish life in medieval Vienna. The museum would thus also provide access to the subterranean excavations. In view of their achievements (as cited above), Jakornegg & Pálffy were commissioned to take on the project and to design the square as well. The choice proved to be very fortunate.

**The Design**
As in Kassel previously, the architects began by putting things in order. The old vaults and walls were whitewashed, a monolithic coating of irregular texture covered the floor, and simple cubic glass-and-oak furniture was made for the cash desk, the shop and the exhibits. The architectural design for the museum rooms, numbering five in all, was limited to a few elements and colours: wall, ceiling, floor, (indirect) light and shadow, the warm grey of the fair-face concrete, the irregular texture of the screed flooring, the ephemeral quality of the glass, and the shimmering reflection of the special steel. And, above all: emptiness. The architecture demands and encourages concentration and attention. The exhibits – for example, a model of a medieval town, the multimedia documentation containing data on more than 65,000 murdered Austrian Jews, and Rachel Whiteread's design sketches – are supposed to speak, and not serve as mimetic architectural gestures.

Nevertheless, the stairs to the basement-level rooms and the corridor leading to the

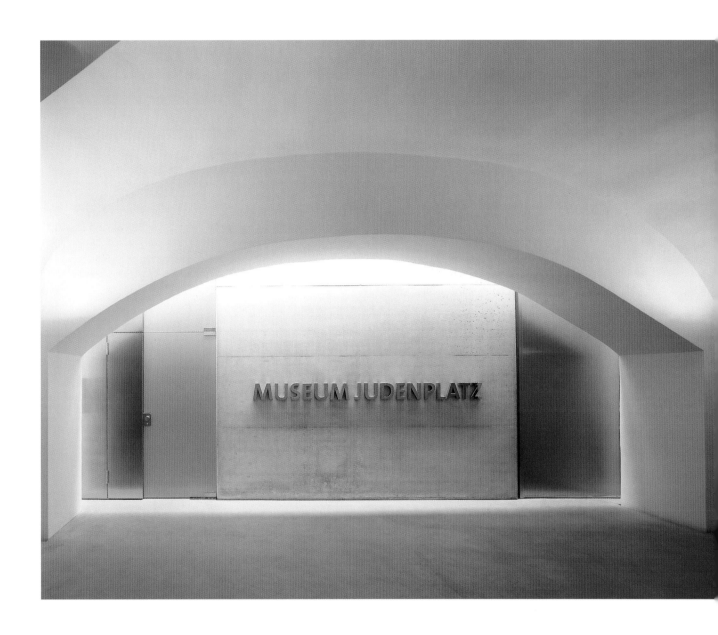

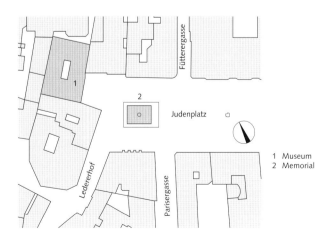

Location plan 1:2,500

When planning the exhibition buildings, the architects conceived the architecture above all as a space enclosed by planes, one in which flat elements became spatially effective.

The walls, ceiling and floor are accentuated by indirect lighting.

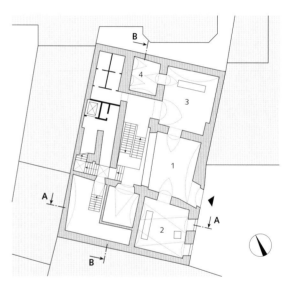

Ground floor 1 : 750

Access to the memorial centre in the second basement floor of the museum.

1 Foyer
2 Exhibition
3 Information
4 Document archives of the Austrian Resistance Movement
5 Passageway
6 Soil

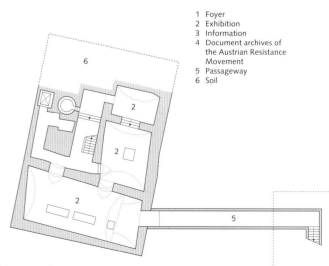

2. Second basement floor, 1 : 750

archaeological excavations create an almost mystical atmosphere: the mysterious light issuing from cracks, and from a seemingly unknown source, falls on a sculpture composed of different planes that has been inserted in the stairwell and makes no secret of its rational character. Encountering the stairwell, one is reminded of Paul Valéry's "Eupalinos or the Architect": "But all these subtleties, which are intended to assure the building's permanence, were nothing compared with those he employed to prepare the sensations and vibrations that were supposed to arise in the soul of a future observer of his work."

Thus prepared and guided through a long concrete tube, the visitor to Judenplatz Museum arrives via stairs – ascending this time – at the foundations of the destroyed synagogue. And in this dark room, he is alone with these foundations and his memories. The architects' intervention is limited to providing a setting for the memory: the dark-red pigmentation of the clay ground with its steel mesh, the galvanised brass-plate bowl defining the limits of the excavation, the ceiling lights which are directed solely at the walls. Only gradually does one become aware of the two rooms, the bimah (the raised platform from which the Torah is read out), and the floor. The past and the present are strictly separated. Yet it is a place the visitor remembers. Together, Whitehead, with her upside-down bookshelves in the square above, and Jabornegg & Pálffy, with their sensitively displayed excavations, have created a unity of remembrance.

View of the memorial centre where a synagogue once stood.

**Building data**

| | |
|---|---|
| Building | Judenplatz Museum |
| Location | Judenplatz 8, 1010 Vienna, Austria |
| Client | City of Vienna represented by the Historisches Museum der Stadt Wien |
| Completion | 2000 |
| Specialists | Dipl.Ing. Öhlinge & Metz, structural design, Vienna |
| | Dipl. Ing Dr. Karlheinz Wagner, structural design, Vienna |
| | Dipl. Ing Walter Prause, building physics, Vienna |
| | C°E Planungs-Ges. m.b.H., service installations, Vienna |
| | Landschaftsarchitekten Teuttsch Ritz Rebmann, landscaping, Munich |
| Size of plot | 402 m² |
| Floor area | 797.76 m² |
| Construction cost | Approx.€ 8,117/m² (incl. the design of the square) |

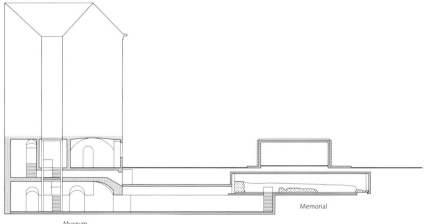

Museum  Memorial

**Section AA 1:750**

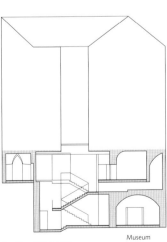

Museum

**Section BB 1:750**

# Extension to the Centre PasquArt in Biel, Switzerland

Architects: Diener & Diener Architects, Basel

The striking feature of this project, which is situated in the gorge between the soaring Jura Mountains and the lakeside town of Biel, is already present in the topography of the site. The building enjoys a rare status, one that lends it an intrinsic forcefulness, precisely by virtue of its location between these two defining features. If one views the building from the front, i.e. facing its shop windows on the street side, one gets the impression that it has been designed solely to face the street. There it stands in its neutral grey stony concrete suit: natural stone falling into line, like a new neighbour, with the venerable warm sandstone and ochre stucco of the adjacent structures. The building seems rather heavy and awkward, perched there on one leg as though undecided about whether to remain or not.

As one moves round the house, however, one becomes aware that it also opens onto the mountain slope and thus relates to the existing town hospital and the old-people's home. On the side facing the open, undeveloped countryside and the rising Jura ranges beyond, all the clumsiness vanishes, and monstrosity gives way to the sense of a sculpture placed here as a categorical marker of the town's boundary.

Entering the shop-window façade, one feels rather lost at first. Surrounded by large, continuous glass fronts, one can look back onto both the street and the colourful wall, comprising part retaining wall, part artefact, and part Jura rock.

The visitor senses the building's precarious state of equilibrium: not just because it is positioned between town and countryside, but also because he is reminded of this state of affairs no matter where he is in the building. In the new galleries on the first floor, the traditional alignment has been abandoned: the side light entering through the storey-high windows is cast on the front end of the rooms, seeming to set them in motion, despite the tranquillity established by their proportions.

The only room that is both conventional and familiar is the skylit hall, into which light enters unhindered throughout the day. There is an exciting interplay here between the moving light and the tranquil room. The new rooms were not intended merely to supplement the existing rooms: rather, old and new were supposed to sustain and mutually accentuate one another. The stairs of the town hospital provide a key to a spatial system that directly links the old and new parts of the Centre PasquArt in a manner that also mobilises an array of interrelationships. The PasquArt could be read as a metaphor for the town in the flow of time: the existing structure assigns the new a place, yet the new ultimately preserves the status quo. And for all their disequilibrium, the one sustains the other.

**Natural stone optics - it is concrete, after all: sandblasted.**

+ 4.51

1
2
3
4

1   Concrete façade, sandblasted
    on the visible face
2   200 mm air
3   100 mm insulation
4   250 mm concrete

+ 0.00

Façade section 1:50

# Art Museum Liechtenstein in Vaduz

Architects: ARGE Morger, Degelo, Kerez, Basel/Zurich

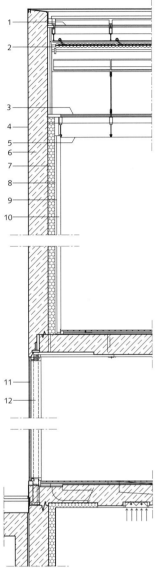

**Façade section 1:75**

1 Glass roof
2 Lamellae providing
  sunshading
3 Glass ceiling with walkabout
  area
4 Ground surface
5 Dust shield
6 Fair-face concrete
7 Foamed glass
8 Air space
9 All-gypsum baseboard
10 Lime plastering
11 Structured glass
12 All-steel support (set in
   window frame)

A mirror is being held up to Vaduz, the capital of Liechtenstein. The rapid transformation of a small farming village into a financial metropolis has left its mark. The dark façade of the new art museum impressively reflects the silhouette of the city against the mountains in the background. Even so, it is not the effect of distant images that gives the building such a vivid appearance, but its velvety surface, which at close range could be mistaken for dark terrazzo, and which awakens a desire to touch the stone. The combination of dark basalt chips and light pebbles from the bed of the Rhine lend the concrete its unforgettable character and at the same time integrate it marvellously into the surroundings. To achieve this shiny effect and render the individual constituents visible, ten grinders had to remove 5–7 mm from the rough façade before it could be sealed. Not the slurry customarily used in fair-face concrete, but the inner-life of the material – and hence its actual bearing structure – has been made visible here. A mobile cement plant was needed to prevent the concrete from segregating during manufacture and pouring. The concrete mix was first tested on a model construction until cracking no longer exceeded 0.3mm. Finding the correct concrete composition was a very instructive process, especially as the form of the aggregates deviated from the ideal spherical shape. The formwork had to be made absolutely impermeable in a few operations. In order to avoid shoulders, it was decided to use 8-metre-high concrete heads. The model construction revealed that the surface would have to be primed and care taken to avoid both rock pockets and segregation. The resulting building called to mind a huge stone monolith, reluctant to reveal its innermost treasure.

The façade has openings on three sides to allow adequate sidelight to penetrate the ground floor. The top floor is illuminated by natural light entering through the roof. Anyone who takes the trouble to climb the hill behind the museum as far as the castle will discern the four-part plan reflected in the layout of the skylights. The room arrangement makes full use of the variations in illumination. In addition to the side-lit room on the ground floor, an artificially lit room has been provided for temporary exhibitions. The cafeteria on the ground floor is illuminated by daylight, and invites guests to linger. A broad staircase leads up into the lighter realms of the rooms on the upper floor. Each of these rooms resembles a "white cube" designed to serve the artworks exhibited there. The life within, like that outside, is conspicuously inconspicuous. And it is this very contrast that makes this building so exciting.

Ground and sealed, the concrete façade gleams like polished natural stone.

# The Media Centre in Mannheim, Germany

Architects: Fischer Architects, Viernheim

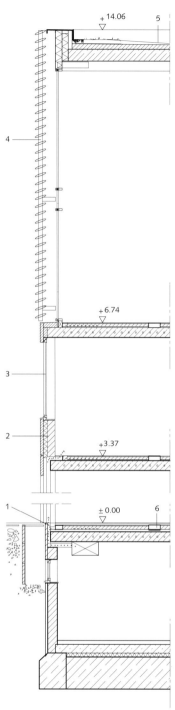

**Vertical section of façade 1:50**

1 Fresh air entering through pipelines
   Waste air released through door
   element
2 Façade element of precast concrete
3 Window element
4 Transom-and-mullion façade
5 Extensively planted roof
6 Continuous electricity duct

What would Jean-August Ingres have said had he discovered his painting *The Source* reproduced on the façade of this media and communications centre? He would probably have been delighted to discover a work dating from his own day in such a fast-moving age. The Media Centre shows that economising wisely does not necessarily relegate artistic additions to a building to second place. Co-operation at an early stage between consultant engineers and architects resulted in a compact building with a sophisticated energy concept. The exterior walls of precast concrete elements were not only designed as load-bearing structures but also carry the ventilation lines. The floors have wide spans, which favours flexible use and also helps keep the rooms cool. The plan is process-orientated, and a large atrium allows for smooth communication between floors. From the outside, strangely enough, one might mistake the place for a bank – except, of course, for Ingres' beauties from classical antiquity, who seem perfectly content to lean against the lamella façade. The artwork portrays a spring that simultaneously serves as a source of inspiration, signalling the theme of the centre to those

outside. "The nymphs at the source are supposed to be Zeus's daughters; as fertility symbols, they are well disposed towards human beings, whom they treat benevolently." The art work was transferred to the façade using the Serilith process. A film is partially covered with surface retarder and placed in the formwork. The areas coming into contact with the surface retarder are then carefully washed. With this process it is possible to reproduce almost any motif on a concrete surface. It can be used with single-layer curtain walls or sandwich elements. The classical motif was a good choice for the Mannheim media centre, whose ground plan is based on traditional atrium typology. Even so, there is a marked contrast between modern construction techniques, which dissolve traditional spatial relations, and this motif taken from a different age.

The images were projected onto the façade using the Serlith procedure.

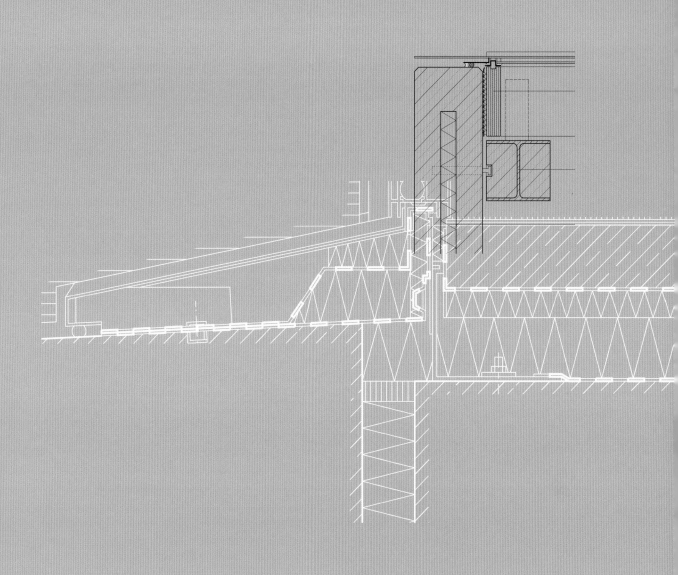

# Building Technology

# Architectural Concrete

**Architect and clients place great demands on the quality of a building and are usually very clear about what they want, especially when it comes to façades. Providers are therefore expected to come up with solutions that combine functionality and aesthetics.**

The development of architectural concrete during the past few years has been a response to such demands. The term architectural concrete refers to concrete whose surfaces have been treated by washing, acid-etching, sand-blasting etc. One of the most interesting fields of application here involves the production of photoengraved, textured, and surface-structured concrete in special processes designed to colour, mould or otherwise enhance the finish of the concrete.

The components used are precast concrete elements such as façade tiles, floors, columns etc., prefabricated for assembly on site. Architectural concrete may be classified according to the procedure involved:
– form/geometry of the building unit
– colour
– surface texture/relief.

### Form/Geometry
Custom-built components are supplied in various sizes and manufactured to a high degree of precision. Dimensions of 3.80 m x 12 m and even greater are available. The fact that concrete is a stable material plays an essential role here.

### Colour
The concrete dyeing process is quite complex. There are scarcely any limits to the colours available. The colour of the concrete components depends on a number of factors: the dye and the dosage added to the cement; the aggregates, which give the concrete a specific hue; and the size and quantity of the aggregates.

### Surface/Relief
The use of architectural concrete permits a variety of surface designs, although it can raise a number of problems too. "Custom-built" solutions are available. While they present a great challenge to a manufacturer's know-how, they nonetheless require years of experience. The spectrum of surface designs ranges from the smooth to the highly textured. Surfaces are characterised by their "concrete skins", which are treated with specific dyes or special effects. With so-called structural concrete, the relief-like structuring of the surface is achieved using special matrixes which are placed in the formwork. The final result also depends on the type and quantity of the cement and aggregates used. In order to obtain special design effects with concrete surfaces, the following processes are used:
– washing
– acid-etching
– sand-blasting
– mechanical (stone-dressing) treatment.

### Washing
When the surfaces are washed, a retarding agent is applied to the concrete. Supplied in liquid form, it is either sprayed or applied with a brush to the formwork. Alternatively, it can be applied as a powder directly to the concrete surface. Retarding agents inhibit or retard the setting of the top layer of cement. Once the concrete has set, the top layer of cement is washed off manually to varying degrees with a hose to expose the granulation in the concrete. A variety of effects can be produced in this way, depending on the form, the mineralogical properties, the size and the colour of the aggregates.

### Acid Etching
Another technique used in designing surfaces is acid etching. In this process, the concrete component is dried and then treated with acid. Two fundamentally different approaches can be distinguished here: acid washing and etching.

In the acid washing process, the concrete is immersed totally in an acid bath. This method is used when the unit is to be treated on all sides.

When the concrete is etched, an acid solution is applied to the surface to be treated, which is then scrubbed mechanically and washed down. This method is particularly suitable for treating clearly defined surfaces. The acid merely removes the cement skin of the unit since it does not deeply penetrate the concrete, exposing only small granules. A variety of effects can be obtained by applying a very precisely calculated acid concentration and strictly adhering to the prescribed application period. After the component has been treated, it is cleaned thoroughly.

The Landzentralbank in Halle: the curtain-wall elements consist of anthracite-coloured, acid-etched concrete. Shiny pebbles, other aggregates, and structured matrixes can be used to create special effects.

Architectural concrete was used to make the "potato stelas" in front of the Federal Chancellery in Berlin.

## Sand-blasting

Sand-blasting is usually employed when matt surfaces are desired. In this process, the surface of the component is sandblasted under high pressure. The granulation is worn down and loses its shine, producing a matt surface. The quality of the surface is determined by varying the processing time and the degree of hardness of the sand in order to expose fine or coarse granulation as desired. In this process, too, the component's surface depends on the properties of the cement, so that the properties of the granulation and the quality of the cement also play an important role.

## Manual Treatment

In addition to the above processes, stonemasonry techniques such as bush hammering, droving, pointing etc. are used. The manual treatment of concrete requires considerable skill, great experience and an intimate knowledge of the material.

Intense co-operation between architects and clients has produced novel solutions for treating architectural concrete. These include photo-engraved concrete and concretes with richly textured surfaces.

## Photoengraved Concrete

Photoengraving provides a method for reproducing photographic images on a concrete surface.

Using a special acid treatment, a permanently insensitive reproduction of any given motif can be generated on a façade without the application of dyes. Specially manufactured plastic foils bearing a motif that has been partly treated with surface retarder are put in the formwork. When the concrete has been placed, the surface is carefully washed.

A variety of surfaces can be produced depending on the choice of cement and aggregate, as well as by washing, acid-etching, sandblasting and mechanical processing.

Photoengraved concrete: many other motifs are conceivable...

# Dyed Concrete as a Sandstone Substitute

**Parts of Dresden central station are being restored using sandstone-coloured concrete. This material is not only relatively inexpensive, but also deceptively similar to the sandstone used for the original building.**

The walls at Dresden central station are being constructed in sections. The south side, 600 m long, has been completed, with work on the north side of the station being resumed in spring 2002. The restored walls will also strengthen the railway embankment, absorbing the compressive load from the trains.

### Reference Wall

There is sandstone and sandstone. As Saxony's traditional stone takes a variety of forms, the concrete specialist had to produce many different shades of colour in his laboratory to create a material deceptively similar to the original. In September 2000, tests began to make an appropriate dyed concrete. This was no easy task, since sandstone ranges in colour from light yellow to dark brown. However, after trying a number of colour mixtures, the first samples were submitted, and a reference wall was produced. The architect and representatives of the historic buildings and monuments office were quite satisfied with the results.

### The Degree of Weathering

As the concrete used here was conceived as a sandstone substitute, the quantities of dye added had to be varied to match the weathering of the original sandstone. A close look at the historical wall now reveals it to be a patchwork of the original historical material and concrete. To ensure an acceptable effect, a quality standard had to be upheld that remained within a close margin of tolerance. This called for people with experience. The manufacturing company has been working with concrete for thirty years, and was involved in testing the use of dyed concrete with precast units back in the days of the German Democratic Republic. In 1992-93 this company even processed sandstone-coloured concrete near the central station. The problem was, however, that nobody knew the composition or the

manufacturer of the pigment that had been used at the time. All that anyone could remember was that they had employed a powder dye. It now remained to establish whether pigment powder was absolutely necessary to attain the desired effect, and to find a company that supplied this type of dye. A suitable partner was finally found who tested all kinds of dyes and consistencies, including granular material and liquid dyes. Fortunately, after only a few attempts, a dye was produced that did without titanium white, which is a very expensive ingredient.

### Seven Tests with Specimens

It took no less than seven tests using different types of dye to find the right one. Powdered dye proved unsuitable because it was both exceedingly difficult to mix and failed to produce a uniform hue. The dye finally selected was found after testing liquid pigments. The concrete shade produced was close to the original. The result obtained with these pigments after short mixing periods was even better than that attained with powdered dye. Furthermore, it was now possible to fulfil the requirements of the ZTV-K Concrete (Central Ordinance for Works of Architecture - Concrete).

After conducting extensive tests, a suitable dye was found for the concrete used to pour the coping on the historical wall. Even then, some technical problems had to be solved to ensure that the process ran according to plan. For example, care had to be taken to use uniform aggregates and cement, since any subsequent changes would have had a noticeable effect on the final colour. Furthermore, the colour of the cement can be a problem if it dominates that of the concrete. After all, a central goal here was to mix and pour the individual ingredients to produce sandstone-coloured concrete. Nor was the colour itself the only consideration: an overall appearance true to the original also called

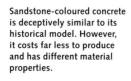

Sandstone-coloured concrete is deceptively similar to its historical model. However, it costs far less to produce and has different material properties.

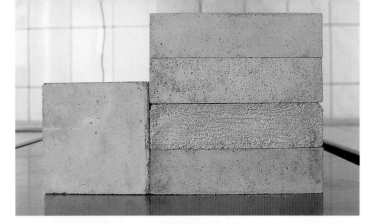

for an identical surface texture. The process was complicated by the fact that it was only possible to pour 30 to 70 cubic metres of concrete with the required sandstone-concrete mix; for the complex 15 to 20 cm thick walls and copings this quantity fell to a mere 5 to 10 cubic metres. Such small quantities made placement a lengthy process, whereas for a load-bearing wall section the 30 cubic metres were quickly processed, taking only about 90 minutes. A test laboratory was also involved in the production process, conducting cube tests and compressive strength tests on the concrete, as well as testing and analysing the uniformity of the air-entrainments, the colour of the concrete, and its consistency and workability. The dye made the concrete a little more viscous. As long as the concrete was fresh, it was easy to compact. As soon as it began to harden, its viscosity and increasing stiffness prevented sufficient quantities of air from escaping from the upper concrete layers. As this process caused so-called blowholes to form, the concrete had to be vibrated for a much longer time than scheduled.

## The Air-Entrainment Ratio Meets DIN Requirements

Even when the dye and surface matched the original, the material properties of the concrete still had to be considered. A problem arose here with respect to air-entrainment, which is necessary to ensure resistance to de-icing salt: the mixers had to add less air-entrainment agent than would be necessary with "normal" concrete, because the "sandstone dye" had already changed the reaction of the individual ingredients. In the first trials, the concrete still contained too much air to develop the required strength. However, the air-entrainment ratio prescribed by DIN was finally obtained by varying the doses of the individual ingredients. Whereas the normal proportion ranges between 0.25 and 0.3 per cent, the proportion here only made up 0.12 per

Above: the quantities of pigment admixed depends on the degree of weathering.

Left: traditional pumps and dosing devices are unsuitable for admixing dye.

cent of the cement content. Where the concrete for the coping had to be poured, air-entrainments (which also depended on the size of the grains) had constituted between 5 and 6.5 per cent of the cement concrete.

According to the manufacturer, clients must expect to pay approximately 25 per cent more for dyed concrete. Any further changes made to the dyed concrete, which automatically necessitate new tests, can push up the price considerably. Conversely, smaller quantities of dye can depress the price. However, the dye is not the sole, decisive factor affecting the total cost.

# Cost-Cutting Assembly

**In the construction industry there is a great need to examine and introduce measures to cut costs whilst preserving current quality standards. One way to reduce operating costs is to reconsider processes.**

One of the biggest cost items in building construction is costed time. This is derived, on the one hand, from wages, including incidental wage costs, and, on the other, from the construction period. If operative time can be significantly shortened, a considerable reduction in costs will result.

The time required to complete trades should always be optimised to the greatest degree possible, with the sequence of the trades being optimised by construction management systems to avoid paying heavy penalties for nonperformance. In many cases, however, the tasks of the individual trades are not directly linked, particularly when no general plan exists to coordinate the interrelated building elements from the moment work starts. Integrative planning can result in considerable savings, however. The patented (DE 100 60 449) front fast system (FFS) offers a means for integrating the various trades. It is based on the idea that the work of reinforcing concrete ceilings, walls and floors need not wait until the shell has been erected, but that reinforcement should be carried out while the concrete is being poured.

The system offers cost-effective solutions for the following reinforcement areas:

For the façades:
– façade units for the exterior and the interior
– down-pipes, lighting conductors, empty conduits for the telephone and power lines, ventilation shafts
– heat insulation and weather-proofing, window and door elements, grilles, gratings etc.

For the interior walls:
– empty conduits for power and communications lines,
– ventilation shafts, wall cladding, cupboard and shelf systems, fittings etc.

For the ceilings:
– elements for false ceilings
– ducts for power and communications lines
– lighting installations
– sprinklers, water lines
– air-conditioning systems
– ventilation ducts
– any ceiling conveying equipment etc.

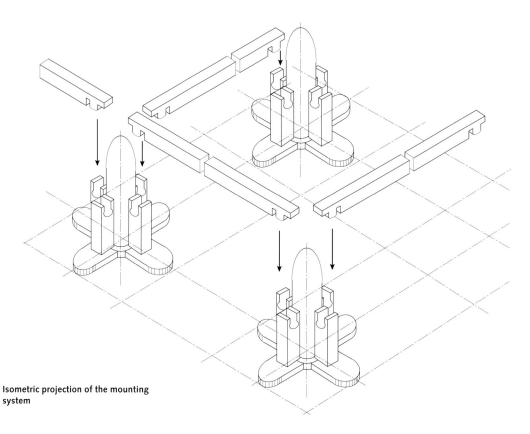

Isometric projection of the mounting system

### The Idea

In industrial and commercial buildings (including offices), a minimum or standard set of such installations is necessary. The necessary connections – above all, dowels – can be prepared and installed while the shell is being erected. Consequently, a simple way must be found to fit the dowels to the shuttering without any great expenditure of time, and to dimension them so that all the envisaged connections are in position and immediately accessible after the shuttering is removed.

### The System

FFS is a modular and highly flexible system of dowels and tie bars. The dowels have standardised, cross-shaped baseplates; the tie bars are made of plastic. The dowels and tie bars are linked and interlocked with one another as desired with simple notch-and-plug components.

A reinforcing grid is thus created into which the planned reinforcements can be bolted. Dowels of different sizes, materials, load-bearing capacities etc., are used to take into account specific loads. The length of the baseplates and the bars corresponds to that of the distance washers normally used for the reinforcement encasement. Their use renders distance washers superfluous.

The dowel elements – baseplates and bars – are supplied with adhesive foils on both sides so that they can be attached without tools to the casting slab or shuttering. The foils also prevent the concrete paste from entering the dowel apertures, thus ensuring that the latter remain clean. The foils can be left in place and pierced later when needed.

If one follows this procedure, the poured surfaces remain completely smooth and can be processed without any further preliminary treatment. The differences in the load-bearing capacity of the dowels are identified by foils of varying colour so that they can be unequivocally identified even after a long period.

As they are set during pouring, the dowels sit far more firmly in the matrix than would be possible if they were pushed into drilled holes. Consequently, where loads are equal, smaller dowels can be used than with traditional systems.

### On Site

FFS reinforcements render all drilling work unnecessary, thus saving wear and tear on drills and bits.

There is no longer any overhead work, and the noise and dust caused by drilling is eliminated.

All the preparation and work that drilling requires, including marking the positions of the boring holes, is eliminated.

As the surfaces can no longer be chipped by drilling, the poured surfaces remain perfectly intact.

There is no more corrosion due to reinforcements being damaged and exposed during drilling.

The reinforcements can no longer be damaged during drilling as the dowels are placed prior to reinforcement; furthermore, the reinforcements do not have to compete with the dowels for space.

Thanks to the basic grid, special dowels with the most varied forms can be used as desired for predefined uses.

By using the basic grid, the spaces between the dowels remain constant; deviations can be kept to <1 cm without any problem whatsoever.

Construction delays no longer occur due to failure to co-ordinate trades, or through weather-induced disruptions.

As soon as the concrete has set and the shuttering has been removed the planned installation work can be completed, thus saving much waiting time.

If enough dowels are set in the grid, subsequent installation work can be performed easily without any need for further drilling.

Standardisation of the grid facilitates the manufacture of installation elements, allowing serial (and hence lower-cost) production.

### Costs

From the standpoint of overall costs, it is evident that this system can result in considerable savings proportionate to the scale of the necessary wall, ceiling and floor installations. The only problem entailed is the organisational need to co-ordinate in advance all the various trades involved in construction so that appropriate planning leads to the desired savings. Foresight here is not limited to the construction period, but can also be extended to include subsequent fitting-out work, so that the above-mentioned advantages may be reaped again when repairs are undertaken or further equipment is installed.

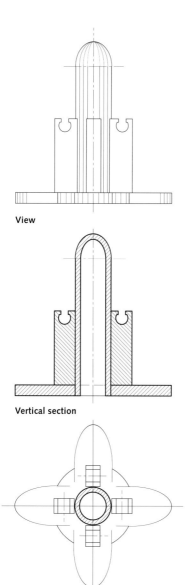

View

Vertical section

Horizontal section

# Thin Glassfibre-Reinforced Concrete Structures

**Non-reinforced, cement-bound concretes have a high compressive strength and low tensile strength. As the matrix forms a brittle load-bearing material, it can suddenly fail without advance warning even if only slight deformation occurs.**

Consequently, (steel) reinforced concrete components subject to bending forces must have a minimum degree of reinforcement. In other words, there must be sufficient concrete cover to prevent the reinforcing steel from corroding and to bond the steel and concrete. With steel-reinforced concrete, it is not possible to construct components subject to bending forces if they have an overall thickness of less than 3 cm.

Very thin fibre-reinforced concrete components can be manufactured by adding suitable fibres – e.g. short fibres embedded as uniaxial fibre strands or as flat fabrics. Taking the example of glassfibre-reinforced concrete, we shall examine possible manufacturing processes and fields of application for thin-layer building products made of (glass) fibre-reinforced concrete to convey an idea of the material properties of fibre-reinforced concrete in general.

## Glassfibre-Reinforced Concrete as a Building Material

### – Cement-bound matrix

The addition of glass fibres significantly changes the stress-strain behaviour of concrete, which is a rigid cement-bound material. The fibres hinder cracks from opening inside the hardened cement paste, whilst ensuring that any cracks that do appear are equally distributed. The preconditions for this are an equal distribution of fibres and an adequate fibre-matrix bonding. The same principles apply to the composition of glassfibre concretes and mortars as to fibreless concretes.

### – Aggregates

The maximum grain size of the aggregates must be adjusted to the thickness of the building elements and the fibre lengths. To ensure homogeneous bearing behaviour, the maximum grain size diameter must not exceed 4 mm. The proportion of sands (close to grading curve B) must be increased, otherwise concrete tends to bleed. The aggregates-cement ratio depends on the manufacturing procedure and the desired bearing behaviour.

### – The water-cement ratio

Water-cement ratios of between 0.35 and 0.50 are used. As the water-requirement of glassfibre-reinforced concrete rises with any increase in the surface to be covered, fluidisers or wetting agents are recommended here.

### – The cement content

The cement content of glassfibre-reinforced concrete and mortars for thin building components depends on the following influencing variables:

| Glassfibre-reinforced concrete type | Cement content [kg/m] |
| --- | --- |
| Glassfibre-reinforced mortar | 400-700 |
| Glassfibre-reinforced concrete for thin building elements | 600-800 |
| Pure cement-paste matrix | Approx. 1,200 |
| Hatschek process | Approx. 700 to 800 |

To improve alkali resistance, the addition of organic binders (e.g. polymer) and/or the partial substitution of fly ash for cement is also recommended.

## Fibres

Unlike other fibres (e.g. steel fibres), AR-glass fibres are bundles of fibres comprising between

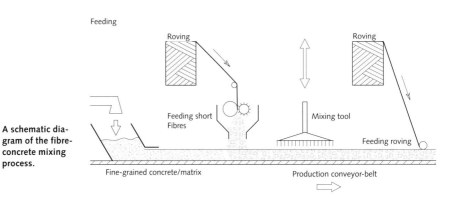

A schematic diagram of the fibre-concrete mixing process.

Feeding

Roving

Feeding short Fibres

Fine-grained concrete/matrix

Roving

Mixing tool

Feeding roving

Production conveyor-belt

around 100 and 200 single filaments with a diameter of approximately 10 to 15 μm. During the past few years, a large range of glassfibre products has been developed which differ with respect to both the number of single filaments and the number of layers used. For example:
– rovings (glassfibre strands comprising 32 filaments, of any length desired)
– glassfibres with 102 or 204 filaments in various lengths of between 6 and 25 mm and with varying sizings, which dissolve into single filaments on contact with water (use as process fibres, improved homogeneous distribution in the matrix, improved stability of green concrete)
– glass fibre mats (chopped strand mat – CSM), newly developed glass fibre mats made of AR glass fibres approximately 50 mm long, bonded with a binder, form a non-aligned two-dimensional fibre mesh. The load-bearing capacity and ductility of the reinforced glass-fibre concrete can be increased by using CSMs.

### Load-bearing Behaviour
The basic difference in the bearing behaviour of fibrated concrete as compared with conventional concretes becomes apparent when the matrix reaches breaking strength. Fibres in the matrix function as (micro) bridges across the cracks. The post-cracking behaviour of fibrated concrete can fulfil two functions:
1. It can raise the breaking strength and the elongation at fracture of the fibrated concrete in load-bearing building components that do not have conventional reinforcements.
2. It can increase the viscosity and improve the workability of the fibrated concrete by activating and extending the fibres in a (micro) crack area in non-bearing building components and in those with conventional reinforcements.

The requirements in item 1 can only be satisfied using supercritical fibre-reinforced concretes and mortars. The critical fibre content $V^{f,crit}$ of a concrete or mortar matrix can be defined as a function of the fibre length and diameter as follows: as the fibre content at which the fibres are able to absorb the additional forces from the matrix $\sigma_m$ $AV_m$ without their being stretched.

The critical fibre content $V_{f,crit}$, and, therefore, the required minimum fibre content needed to produce ductile material behaviour increase when the fibre diameter and matrix breaking strength are greater, and the bonding capacity of the fibre matrix and fibre length are reduced.

### The Durability of Glassfibre Concrete
Two corrosion mechanisms are responsible for the progressive decline in both ductility (especially of elongation at fracture) and the ultimate shearing stress of the glassfibre-reinforced concrete under bending tension and tensile stress:
1. The glass fibres are corroded chemically due to the high alkalinity of the paste matrix. The $OH^-$ ions in the alkaline solutions split the oxygen bridges in the glassfibre construction, forming calcium hydrosilicate and thereby destroying the silicon-oxygen-skeleton.

The precondition for initiating this process is an aqueous solution with a pH value of >9. In comparison with conventional E-glass fibres, alkali-resistant glass fibres are very resistant to chemical corrosion.

To safeguard against corrosion, the following measures can be taken:
– using AR-glass types with a high zirkonium content. $ZrO_2$ has the effect of forming insoluble surface layers composed of hydrated zirconium oxide. These layers have a protective function.

68

Thin glassfibre-
reinforced elements
as an acoustic sail.

– applying an additional coating (skim coat) to the AR glass fibres to reduce chemical corrosion.
– using cement-bound slurries that that will have only a very small calcium hydroid content after a few months (pH value <9).

2. In contrast to steel and plastic fibres, embedded glass fibres are not single glass fibres, but strands composed of single filaments completely coated with sizing.

The accumulation of calcium hydroxide crystals on the fibre surface progressively restricts the moveability of the fibre bundles and the single filaments in relation to one another. As these fibre bundles fuse, the glassfibre concrete becomes more brittle and loses strength. Special sizings can be used with more modern AR glass fibres to change the surface structure. There is a greater quantity of porous CSH fibres and fewer crystalline CH fibres, which cause the fibres to become brittle, among the single filaments.

During the past few years, special, more durable matrixes have been developed: e.g. by adding fly ash or micro-silica, using polymer-modified matrixes, hydraulic binders etc.

**Manufacturing Processes for Thin Glassfibre-Reinforced Concrete Building Elements**

The method chosen for manufacturing building products made of glassfibre-reinforced, cement-bound slurries depends on:
– the type of product
– the type of fibre (fibre length, fibre content etc.)
– the quantity to be produced
– the technical requirements placed on the building products.

The following is a brief presentation of the most important manufacturing processes.

*Mixing*
The short glass fibres are usually added to the premixed matrix. Care must be taken not to exceed the remaining mixing time of approximately 30 seconds, otherwise the glass fibres can fray. As is customary with concretes and mortars, further processing generally involves spraying the matrix or pouring it into moulds. The addition of fibres (max. 2% vol., fibre length 6 to 25 mm) makes processing more difficult and increases the water requirement. Plasticisers and fluidisers are recommended.

*Spraying*
In the so-called fibre-spraying process, short fibres made from rovings in a fibre-cutting plant are sprayed into position using compressed air. Together, the fibres and the cement-bound matrix are sprayed continuously onto the form-creating surface (shuttering). Additional compression can be obtained by rolling, vibrating or pressing the matrix to improve the fibre-matrix bond. The fibres are usually aligned two-dimensionally; the fibre content comprises up to approximately 5% vol.). The spraying process is used for manufacturing large flat construction surfaces (e.g. façade elements).

*The Hatschek Process*
In this process, an aqueous slurry is made of fibres (fibre cocktail of cellulose [process fibres] and glass fibres) and then placed in a rotating sieve cylinder. The mix then passes onto felt conveyor belts. These dehydrate and harden the paste, which passes through rolling presses, producing a thin sheet which can then be rolled. This process is repeated until the desired thickness is obtained. The components produced (corrugated sheets, flat panels) are then hardened in steam chambers. The bonding strength of the cellulose fibres ensures that no cement particles are washed out (filtering effect).

*The Wellcrete Process*
The Wellcrete process, like the Hatschek process, is suitable for the continuous series production of thin large-sized glassfibre components (corrugated sheets, flat panels). In contrast to the Hatschek process, this method
– does not rely on excess water
– permits the embedding of short glass fibres in areas subject to considerable stress
– permits the embedding of additional aligned glassfibre rovings.

**Fields of Application of Building Products Made of Glassfibre-Reinforced Concrete**
**The Requirements of the Construction Supervisory Authorities**

In Germany, the guidelines on building products and the current Land building regulations classify glassfibre-reinforced concrete building products as follows:
1. Building components where the safety of load-bearing elements plays an essential role (construction regulation list A), for example corrugated sheets for roofing, slab façades, prefabricated façades, gypsum ceiling base-board, components for balcony parapets etc.

A permit from the construction supervisory authorities is usually required before these prefabricated products, which must also pass special tests, can be used. A permit is also required in each specific case for the use of a new building product (e.g. glassfibre-reinforced concrete shells as load-bearing structures).

2. Building elements where the safety of load-bearing elements plays a secondary role (building regulation list C), such as small fibrated-concrete slabs, window ledges, drainage gutters, building elements where the safety of load-bearing elements is only of temporary interest (e.g. integrated formwork), building components that meet the requirements of building regulations list A, in which the addition of glass fibres merely improves utility or durability (e.g. glassfibre-reinforced screeds and plasters, fireproofing panels, mortar for maintenance work etc.).

**Examples**
Passing over for the moment the best-known glassfibre-reinforced-concrete building components – prefabricated corrugated sheets and flat slabs (used for roofing and façades) – let us briefly examine a few lesser-known applications for such building components.

*Parapet slabs, folded plates*
Individual moulding is possible when the components are poured or sprayed. Industrial scale production is not absolutely necessary. Architects are often disturbed by the smooth surfaces of glassfibre-reinforced concrete. Fall-proof parapet slabs with both rough surfaces and washed-concrete textures are also available.

*Glassfibre-reinforced-concrete shells*
A special field of application of sprayed glassfibre-reinforced-concrete is the manufacture of thin-walled shell load-bearing systems. As early as 1977, a glassfibre-reinforced-concrete shell with a span of 31 m and a shell thickness of 10 to 14 mm was manufactured for the German Garden Exhibition in Stuttgart.

*Large-format load-bearing slabs*
Large-format load-bearing slabs of concrete are frequently used for gypsum ceiling baseboards for ventilated stucco façades. To give the stucco façade a seamless appearance, glassfibre-reinforced concrete slabs are used with minimal shrinkage and deformation behaviour to prevent cracking at the rendered slab joints. An interesting alternative for ventilated external wall cladding consists in the use of flat glassfibre-reinforced concrete slabs on a steel-frame substructure, which provides a base for factory-mounted ceramic cladding.

*Shell components*
Structures with a high load-bearing capacity can be made using folded plates of glassfibre-reinforced concrete. In bridge construction, these components are deployed as integrated formwork. Furthermore, the highly concentrated glassfibre-reinforced concrete fabric offers the reinforcements greater protection against corrosion. The concrete sheathing can be reduced.

**Conclusion**
The addition of fibres can change the rigid material behaviour of concrete in such a way that it can be used for components under great bending stress, thus eliminating the need for additional steel-reinforced concrete. The ductile behaviour of glassfibre-reinforced concrete makes it highly suitable for manufacturing thin building components for façades, roofs and floors, as well as for secondary building products (gutters, window ledges, façade shingle etc.).

# Manufacturing Shell Structures with Sprayed Concrete

**Sprayed concrete can be used to construct extremely fine shell structures. This process calls for a very high degree of skill and careful execution.**

Shell load-bearing structures are primarily used for constructing roofs with wide spans or in industry to manufacture silos and other kinds of storage containers. Concrete has a number of advantages: it can be formed into an infinite number of shapes, has a low material cost and a high compaction strength. However, concrete is only economically viable for manufacturing shells when they are so formed as to transfer most of the external loads and normal stresses. The erection of such shells, with their extreme curvature, requires very costly conventional double-side formwork.

Vibration-compacted concrete can only be poured in single-side formwork for angles not exceeding approximately 30°, so double-side formwork is necessary for greater angles. However, the sprayed-concrete process makes it possible to produce thin shells of any angle and curvature with single-side formwork.

In the case of large building components, this method has the advantage of allowing the manufacture of long-span, double-curvature load-bearing shell structures with minimal formwork. If necessary, an auxiliary structure of steel profiles can be used as a load-bearing reinforcement that is integrated into the final structure.

This mode of construction is obviously not limited to dome structures with double-curvature shells. By spraying the concrete onto a fine wire mesh fixed to the reinforcement, shell structures of all possible shapes and sizes can be made, with or without formwork.

## The Method

Sprayed concrete, as the name suggests, is a type of concrete (produced in accordance with the relevant standards) sprayed with an air-gun onto a surface. Unlike normal concrete manufacturing processes in which the fresh concrete is mixed before the ready mix is poured by conveyors into shuttering for compaction, the concrete spraying process combines all these operations so that they take place simultaneously. A pre-mix, which is only partly prepared, is blasted through a hose and then mixed with the remaining fresh concrete components as it shoots through the hose nozzle. It is then simultaneously placed and compacted. During spraying, some of the shot rebounds, changing the original mixture. Hence,

in some respects, the manufacture of sprayed concrete differs considerably from the manufacture of normal concrete. Furthermore, only trained nozzle operators may be employed for this spraying concrete, and they have to know the relationships between the composition of the pre-mix, the quantity of the shot rebounding, and the properties of the spayed concrete once it has been placed. For this reason, the use of sprayed concrete in areas with very high technical requirements tends to be the domain of specialised contractors possessing both the necessary know-how and the latest machinery.

Sprayed concrete is applied in dry and wet spraying processes. These two processes are distinguished by the composition of the premix and the spraying equipment. In the dry spraying process, the premix is composed of sandy gravel and cement conveyed by a thin stream of compressed air through the hose to the nozzle. Only there, in a mixing chamber, is the required quantity of mixing water added.

With wet-process sprayed concrete, the premix already contains the mixing water. The mixture is shot through the hose in a dense stream. Some guns use compressed air to shoot the mixture in a thin stream. In the dense-stream method, compressed air must be added to churn up the shot and generate the necessary impact energy so that the spray mixture will remain bonded to the surface.

The German industrial standard DIN 18551, sprayed concrete, applies to both processes. Sprayed concrete produced under this standard is defined as concrete in accordance with DIN 1045, which means that all the regulations relating to concrete technology basically apply here too. Observation of these rules alone is not, however, a sufficient condition for producing high-quality sprayed concrete, because the conveying and placing technology used in this method form an integral part of the manufacturing process and therefore have a significant influence on the final properties of the concrete. In the manufacture of sprayed concrete, most of the mixing is done in the nozzle, in front of the nozzle, and even on the sprayed surface. The composition of the concrete is therefore determined to an equal degree by the pre-mix, the actual spraying process and, above all, by the nozzle operator. In some respects, the DIN 18551 methods standard thus imposes far higher requirements on execution and quality assurance than DIN 1045.

The recipes for the pre-mix depend on the requirements placed on the hardened concrete and on the prevailing spraying conditions. Although the general laws of concrete technology apply to the effect of the concrete composition on the properties of the hardened concrete, it is important to remember, when designing a spray mix, that the spraying process significantly alters the original concrete composition. Depending on the quantity of rebounding shot – which is influenced, in turn, by the spraying conditions (direction) and the skill of the nozzle operator – very different types of sprayed concrete will be produced by the same concrete mix. The likely rebound quantity must therefore be considered

when designing the premix. As a next step, a preliminary test must be conducted using the designed mix under the likely and anticipated spraying conditions, and the mix changed if necessary.

A 90° angle of impact is optimal for compaction and minimal rebound. Great deviation from this angle will increase the "billiard effect", i.e. coarser grains will penetrate the soft concrete layer with less force. The distance between the nozzle and the spraying surface must be between 0.5 and 1.5 m. If the distance is too short the force of impact will be too high, whereas if the distance is too great, the stream will slow down, causing segregation. It is obviously essential to ensure reasonable spraying conditions; this means, above all, using suitable scaffolding. To reduce rebound, sprayed concrete is increasingly being combined with microsilica. Owing to its chemical and physical effect, microsilica is added to alter both the consistency of the fresh concrete and the setting behaviour of the sprayed concrete. This, in turn, enhances both the mix's processing qualities and its properties as hardened concrete.

Above all, increasing the additive improves the bonding property of the sprayed concrete, thus reducing rebound. The water-binding properties of the very fine microsilica particles speed up the concrete hardening process. Consequently, the concrete can be sprayed in thicker layers,

Fotos: G. Ruffert

**Above: wide-spanning filigree structures are a typical field of application for sprayed concrete.
Below: the nozzle operator's job demands great skill and concentration because it directly affects the composition of the concrete.**

As a matter of principle, sprayed concrete structures are to be manufactured as BII concrete and inspected by an authorised external inspection agency.

eliminating the need for an accelerator and the negative effects of the latter on the concrete's strength. The proportion of rebounding shot, which is extremely high at the start of each new spraying process, declines rapidly once a thickness of 2–3cm has been reached. As a result, thicker layers also reduce rebounding.

Sprayed concrete is very shrink-prone, fulfilling all the parameters known to induce shrinkage: a relatively high proportion of cement and fine grains, and rapid dehydration due to an unfavourable volume/surface ratio. A rough sprayed surface makes the evaporation area 2 to 3 times greater, thus obviously accelerating shrinkage. Great caution is therefore advisable when curing building components manufactured under the sprayed-concrete process.

Faulty sections, especially cracks, can only be avoided if the concrete is cured (kept wet) long and intensively enough to ensure that substantial dehydration and, therefore, shrinkage can only occur after the sprayed concrete has already become sufficiently strong to absorb the tensions that arise when shrinkage is restricted. This state is generally reached after 7 days (depending on the type of cement used and environmental conditions).

During the past few years, there has been progress in the use of sprayed concrete for building curved and relatively thin concrete shells. The most marked developments have been in the area of fibrated concrete.

Sprayed steel-fibre reinforced concrete is a composite material composed of short concrete and short steel fibres batched during the spraying process. The joint action of the paste matrix, which is not very ductile, and the easily formable steel fibres creates a material with completely new properties. The publication of

the new leaflet Stahlfaserbeton und Stahlfaserspritzbeton (Steel-Fibre Reinforced Concrete and Sprayed Steel-Fibre Reinforced Concrete) by the Deutscher Betonverein has boosted the use of steel-fibre concrete, especially for making building elements with complex geometric forms. The high wage costs incurred in installing curved reinforcements for dome vaults can be reduced considerably using steel-fibre reinforced concrete. Under certain circumstances, the three-dimensional distribution of the reinforcements also provides a more favourable basis for calculations. However, there are still no generally applicable design regulations satisfying all the requirements of the German industry standard, DIN 1045 Concrete and Reinforced Concrete. This state of affairs has done much to restrict the use of steel-fibre concrete for structural purposes. It is still not possible to obtain a generally valid permit from the inspector of works for steel-fibre reinforced concrete applications. Permits to use this material must be obtained from the competent building supervisory authority for each separate project.

## Quality Assurance for Sprayed Concrete Applications

A greater number of quality assurance measures have to be performed to guarantee high-quality execution with sprayed-concrete applications than is the case with normal concrete applications. In view of this fact, German industry standard DIN 18551 requires that – independently of the concrete strength grade – sprayed concrete be manufactured, in principle, as B II concrete and inspected by an external testing agency. Both the inspection procedures stipulated in DIN 45 and the requirements presented in detail in the table appended to DIN 18551 specify how contractors and operators are to inspect the execution of their own work. Outside control is to be carried out by an institution authorised to perform B II controls.

## Practical Examples

Sprayed concrete is ideal for thin concrete building components with large areas and for those with complex forms. The possibility of using sprayed concrete to manufacture a shell structure was first explored by a pioneer of steel-reinforced concrete construction, Professor Dischinger, in his design of the Zeiss Planetarium in Jena in 1925. The planetarium was given a sprayed-concrete dome with a span of 40 m and a thickness of only 6 cm.

This method has also been used to construct church roofs and a great variety of self-supporting dome structures. As a rule, the sprayed concrete is applied to permanent formwork and, typically, to closely meshed wire, expanded metal mesh, or Heraklith sheets fixed to steel structures. In some cases, steel structures (needed to shape the form and hold the meshed wire that creates the surface to which the sprayed concrete is applied) have also been used as load-bearing reinforcements in the shell. In other cases, the sprayed concrete shell is formed on earth mounds designed for this purpose, which are removed after the concrete has hardened.

During the last few decades, a series of church and hall roofs with wide spans – such that of the Rochuskirche in Dusseldorf – have been manufactured with sprayed concrete. In the former German Democratic Republic, in particular, sprayed concrete was frequently used to manufacture shell roofs.

Fields of application in which sprayed concrete has proven useful in the past few decades include bobsleigh runs and artificial streams. Sprayed concrete was used to construct the bobsleigh run for the Munich Olympics.

Another application of sprayed concrete is the manufacture of highly irregular, thin-shelled structures such as artificial rocks and climbing-walls. Large sculptures and building elements with structured surfaces are made by spraying concrete onto permanent formwork. One such example is the Goetheanum in Dornach (Switzerland), where the moulded interior elements were created with sprayed concrete that was sculptured on hardening.

The manufacture of load-bearing shell structures with sprayed concrete received a boost when pneumatically inflated formwork came into use. Structures created in this manner have been employed for some time to erect provisional meeting and exhibition rooms. They are made by inflating a balloon of rubber or elastic plastic material. Compressors keep the air pressure in the balloon at the level needed to support the external forms.

It was an obvious next step to use these shells, which are both easy to erect and relatively stable, for creating dome structures or – from the point of view of statics – uniform double-curvature shells.

The required external reinforcement is made in the form of a radial span, using clamping sleeves in some structures, onto which concrete is then sprayed. A relatively fine aggregate and a soft sprayed concrete (preferably wet-process sprayed concrete) is used. It is applied in several operations in rings to prevent the one-sided build-up of loads.

Sprayed concrete can be used to produce all kinds of forms. However, considerable care is required in their execution in situ.

# The Building Structure as an Energy Storage

**The use of natural sources to cool buildings often involves delays and shortages in supply. A suitable storage system is needed to remedy this shortcoming.**

This cooling method makes direct use of the building structure itself, particularly the ceilings and floors managed through a system of embedded plastic pipes containing flowing water. The room ceilings and floors used in conjunction with the building service installations serve as constitutive units in a thermally active building system (tabs). Dimensions are calculated by using time-based simulations.

## Contentment and Comfort

When temperatures are too high or low, human productivity suffers. Consequently, comfortable temperatures are not a luxury, but play a vital part in creating a pleasant working environment. The concept of comfort is complex, and includes physiological parameters and environmental influences as well as sensations that differ from one person to the next. In the 1970s a variety of studies addressed the issue, the best known probably being that conducted by Professor O. Fanger.

Fanger's investigations reveal that the most important factors influencing the human heat balance and thus a person's sense of comfort are the air temperature, the mean temperature of the space-enclosing surfaces, the humidity, the air velocity, and the person's activities and clothing. The dependence of comfort on these six variables is summarised in Fanger's comfort equation, which is based on an extensive experimental study on a large group of subjects.

To be pleasant, room temperature does

not have to be constant but can vary within an appropriated range. In addition, an occupant may also adapt to temperature fluctuations by changing his or her clothing. The heating, ventilation and cooling systems must be dimensioned to allow optimum use of the admissible comfort range and economical use of the required heating and cooling energy.

## The Heat Balance of a Room

Modern building envelopes with very efficient heat insulation have already lowered energy requirements quite considerably, thus creating novel possibilities for heating and cooling rooms. Attention can now be paid therefore to systems based on low-temperature heating and natural cooling. (The all-glass facades now fashionable often cancel out the effect of the improved properties of the glass.)

Solar heat gains still plays a decisive role in supplying heat, especially in the spring, summer and autumn. Room heat is also generated by people, devices and lighting, so that modern office buildings need cooling throughout most of the year. Because the use of natural cold sources generally involves delays and shortages in supply, high external air temperatures generally result in high room temperatures.

Since it is not always possible to use the surrounding air to cool a building, a suitable storage system is required to redress the imbalance between the demand for coolness during the day and its availability at night. Storage systems such as cold-water storage tanks, however, generally occupy a lot of space, and space is costly. Engineers have therefore turned their attention to using the building structure, particularly the ceilings and floors, as a central storage system. Given concrete's high density and specific heat capacity, buildings made of it have a considerable thermal storage capacity. With appropriate management of the building, its mass can be used efficiently, as in any such storage unit, to transform the structure into a thermally active building system.

## Thermally Active Building Systems

The standard way of showing how building management operates is to examine the temperature cycle within a room. Say the room temperature in

Plastic pipes
before concret
casting

the morning is 22°C. The heat gain in the room due to heat sources such as technical equipment, human beings, solar influx through the windows may cause the air and room temperature to rise over the course of the day to, let us say, 26°C. This rise is largely caused due to heat being discharged convectively from these heat sources. The difference between the air and room surface temperatures increases until the convective heat generated by the heat sources has been transferred via the air to these surfaces.

This temperature difference disappears as soon as the heat sources cease to be operative. The thermoactive surfaces become warmer as they continually absorb the energy released by the heat sources. As this occurs, the "building accumulator" is being charged. The air or room temperature does not therefore remain constant in a thermoactive system, but fluctuates within the temperature range established by Fanger. To re-establish the initial temperature the following day, the "building accumulator" has to be discharged, otherwise the initial room temperature will be even higher than it was at the start of the previous day. From the above it is evident that the room temperature can rise over the permissible maximum room temperature depending on how much heat is absorbed. The building heat accumulator is "discharged" by means of water flowing through plastic pipes (the pipe system) embedded in the building structure. 'Discharge' is either effected at night only, or takes place over the course of the entire day. In the latter case, however, the cooling performance is weaker.

The thermally active building system can be used to cool as well as heat the rooms.

**Modelling the Thermally Active Building System**
Various factors have to be taken into account when tracking room temperature over time in a building equipped with thermally active building systems. Temperature is affected on the one hand by the form of construction (glazing, solar protection, flooring) and the heat gain in the room and, on the other hand, by the heating and cooling system. All these factors can only be taken into account by performing a thermal simulation calculation. As the thermally active building system described here uses embedded pipes, a three-dimensional analysis of the heat transfer must be taken into account.

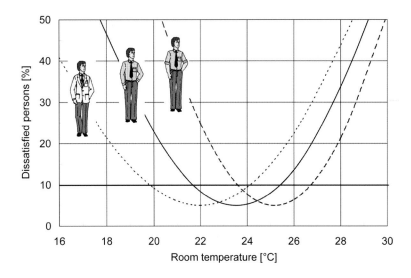

Dependence of dissatisfaction on the room temperature in relation to types of clothing (sedentary work).

There are various methods for computing multi-dimensional heat transfer, two of the most common being finite differences (FD) and the finite element method (FEM). With both methods, the system under consideration is subdivided into three-dimensional grid cells. Calculation takes a long time owing to the (generally) great number of grid points required to perform a precise calculation. Furthermore, experience is required for inputting geometry data and assigning the grid.

The alternative analytical model developed by EMPA uses the stationary differential equation for thermal conduction. With the aid of resistance models, the system's thermal conduction is reduced to a one-dimensional form, which simplifies the calculation considerably.

Analytical presentation also facilitates optimisation of the individual parameters. In addition, thermal simulation programs already contain one-dimensional calculation models and do not therefore require subsequent adjustment. By making a carefully calculated approximation, the developed theory can be extended to include time-based calculations, which play a crucial role in the case of thermally active building systems units due to the enormous mass of the building.

**A Comparison of the Analytical Model with FEM Calculations**
The developed simplified model was tested using time-based FEM calculations.

| Clothing: | Temperature range: |
|---|---|
| Jacket | 20-24°C |
| Shirt | 22-26°C |
| Short-sleeved shirt | 24-27°C |

Admissible temperature range by a max. of 10% dissatisfied people among the room-users questioned.

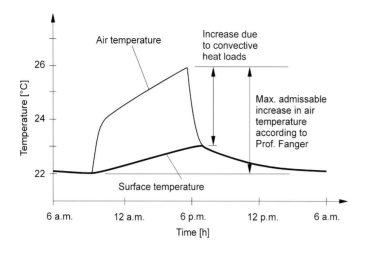

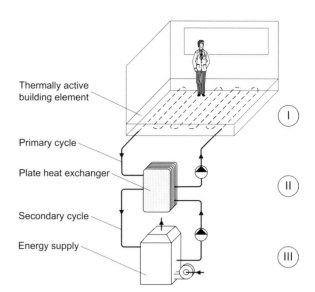

Left: temperature cycle when thermally active building systems are used.

Right: the three-component heat-exchanger model used for the thermally active building system (tabs).

This verified the close correspondence between the model presented and the detailed FEM calculation.

### From the Heat Transfer in the Room to the Energy Supply

Although the pipes embedded in the building element are the most conspicuous feature, they are only one component of the thermally active building system. Overall optimisation of the system involves considering a number of factors ranging from the heat-transfer mechanism in the room to the heating and cooling energy supply.

The thermally active building system consists of three coupled heat exchangers. The first heat exchanger is the thermally active system itself. The second, a plate heat exchanger, separates the water-filled primary cycle from the secondary glycol-filled cycle. The third heat exchanger is the supply of cold. An optimised system can obviously only be created by taking into account all of the components involved in transferring energy. Optimisation entails choosing specific components for the system on the basis of both ecological and economic criteria. A utility value analysis can be undertaken before the final decision is made.

# Activating Concrete

**The use of the low-temperature heating and high-temperature cooling of buildings by means of water-filled pipes integrated into building elements has gained in popularity since the early 1980s.**

In view of the high cost of energy for cooling buildings in many countries, a debate is under way about whether air-conditioning is acceptable or whether there should be legislation restricting its use. Air-conditioning undoubtedly makes it easier to control room temperatures, enhances comfort and leads to higher productivity than is the case with cooled rooms. However, it is well known that people often feel uncomfortable in air-conditioned rooms due to the drafts and the noise generated, and that many suffer from sick building syndrome.

Heating and cooling can also be provided by radiant systems using flowing water, which are operated in conjunction with ventilation systems to supply air of acceptable quality.

This article examines the potential and limits of radiant surface heating and cooling systems, in which pipes are embedded in the floors, walls and ceilings and in the concrete slabs between the storeys. The article also offers recommendations on how to determine the heating and cooling capacity of these systems and discusses appropriate control systems and their construction.

The heating systems generally used in Europe are based on radiators and floor-heating systems and use water as a medium. These systems use radiators and floor heating to generate heat. One advantage they have over air-based systems is that water is a more efficient energy conductor than air. Demands for greater comfort, the improved insulation of buildings, and the greater load produced by users and equipment within buildings have all stimulated greater interest in the installation of cooling systems that maintain room temperatures at a comfortable level. The initial response to these developments was to install suspended ceiling panels for cooling. People subsequently went over to floor-cooling systems and, most recently, to activating the concrete mass of the building.

This last technique, which was inaugurated in Switzerland in the early 1990s, exploits the heat-storing capacity of the concrete slabs between the storeys. Pipes designed to carry flowing water are installed in these concrete slabs to heat and cool the buildings.

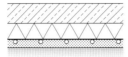

Concrete
Insulation
Plaster
Room temperature

**Ceiling system**

Room temperature
Screed
Insulation
Concrete
Reinforcment

**Thermoactive concrete slab**

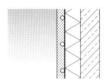

Room temperature
Plaster
Insulation
Concrete

**Wall system**

Room temperature
Flooring
Screed
Insulation
Concrete floor slab

**Floor system**

## Thermal Comfort

Comfort standards can limit the capacity of radiant heating and cooling systems. According to international standards and guidelines (ISO 7730/1994, CR175/1998) the comfort zone for a person performing predominantly sedentary work (1.2 met) lies within an operative temperature range of 20°C to 24°C during the winter (heating period, winter clothing, 1.0 clo) and 23°C to 26°C in the summer (cooling period, summer clothing, 0.5 clo). As the transfer of heat from a heated or cooled surface to a room (or space) and its occupants occurs mainly by means of radiation, it is important to use the operative temperature for computing the comfort conditions and the load. With the activated concrete core system, which exploits the dynamic effects and the thermal storage capacity of the concrete slabs, the operative temperature, which rises over the course of the day, remains within the comfort range. Knudsen (1989) has shown that, provided

The pipes supplying the water are embedded in the concrete slabs between the storeys.

the temperature change remains lower than 5K per hour, the temperature range calculated on the basis of steady state conditions (ISO EN 7730) applies.

Measurements taken with floor-cooling systems reveal that even when the floor temperature falls 10 K below that of the room, the vertical difference in the air temperature between the head and the feet remains below the required value of 3 K. The comfort requirements on the radiant temperature asymmetry are 5 K for heated ceilings and 14 K for cooled ceilings. Consequently, the admissible maximum ceiling temperature is approximately 27°C to 28°C. The admissible minimum ceiling temperature is not limited by the radiant temperature asymmetry, but by the room condensation temperature. The admissible floor temperature for persons wearing shoes ranges from 19°C to 29°C. However, floor temperatures of at least 20°C are recommended in rooms where people generally perform sedentary work.

### The Heating and Cooling Capacity

The factors influencing the heating and cooling capacity of radiant systems are the heat exchange coefficient between the surface and the room, on the one hand, and the admissible maximum and minimum temperatures of the surfaces (based on the room condensation temperature and the heat transfer between the pipes and the surfaces), on the other. The heat exchange coefficient depends on the position of the surface and the surface temperature/room temperature ratio (when heating and cooling). Whereas the radiation heat-exchange coefficient is always approximately 5.5 W/m², the convection heat exchange coefficient varies. The maximum surface temperature cited above for the floor is derived from the European standard for floor heating (EN 1264/1998), which allows the admissible maximum temperature to be increased to 35°C in boundary zones of up to 1m from the external walls. The maximum temperature for wall systems is based on the pain threshold of the human skin, i.e. a temperature of 42°C. The maximum temperature for the ceiling corresponds to the requirement that radiation temperature asymmetry be avoided. The minimum temperatures for wall-and-ceiling systems are determined by the room condensation temperature and the condensation point.

Ceiling systems have the best cooling capacity, whilst floor systems have the better heating capacity. Direct sunlight shining on the floor creates a particular problem as far as floor cooling is concerned. In this case, the cooling capacity of the floor can rise above 100 W/m². This is also a reason why floor cooling is increasingly being used in spaces with large glass areas, as in airports, atriums and entrance halls.

The heat transfer between pipes containing flowing water and the surface is effected via the walls, the ceiling and the floor, and obeys the same physical laws in each case (unless the walls have air spaces). The standard for floor heating (EN 1264/1998) provides the basis for evaluating and computing the capacity of all three surfaces under these conditions. This capacity depends on the distance between the single pipes, the thickness of the material above (below, next to) the pipes, the material used, and the water temperature. Only one other heat exchange coefficient has to be taken into consideration here, namely, when the position of the surface is different for heating than for cooling.

### Activating Concrete

The heating and cooling of rooms by means of pipes filled with flowing water, installed in the concrete slabs between the upper and lower reinforcement, represents a special case.

It is not only the above-mentioned direct, steady cooling and heating capacity of radiant systems that needs considering here, but also the effect of the heat stored in the concrete slabs.

The principle underlying concrete core activation can be demonstrated with a simple simulation programme. In the diagram below, the top graph shows the temperature change over a period of 24 hours in a room with an internal (people, lighting) and external (temperature, solar radiation) load and no cooling. When measurements start at 6 a.m. all temperature values

**Heat-exchange coefficients, recommended maximum and minimum surface temperatures and corresponding maximum heat and cooling capacities.**

| | | Overall heat exchange coefficient [W/m²K] | | Surface temperature [°C] | | Capacity [W/m²] | |
|---|---|---|---|---|---|---|---|
| | | Heating | Cooling | Max. temp. | Min. temp. | Heating | Cooling |
| Floor | Boundary zone | 11 | 7 | 35 | 20 | 165 | 42 |
| | Occupied zones | 11 | 7 | 29 | 20 | 99 | 42 |
| Wall | | 8 | 8 | -40 | 17 | 160 | 72 |
| Ceiling | | 6 | 11 | -27 | 17 | 42 | 99 |

are 20°C. The moment an internal load comes into play, the operative temperature of the room rises. The temperature rises throughout the day until it reaches approximately 26°C at 6 p.m., when the interior load disappears. During the night, the room – no longer subject to the interior load – cools down again. However, the following morning, the average temperature of the room and the concrete ceiling is 21.3°C, in other words 1.3 K higher than it was on the previous day. Hence, the temperature continues to rise with each day that passes.

If, however, the concrete slab is kept at a temperature of 20°C, as shown in the middle graph, the temperatures on the following day will return to the previous day's value. During the course of the day, the average temperature of the concrete slab rises to 21.5°C, before falling again at night.

The bottom graph shows the temperature curve when the concrete slab is cooled to 20°C at the time the room is not being used. The results here are almost identical to those obtained when the room is cooled for 24 hours. The operative temperature is only slightly higher. This is because while the concrete slab is kept at a temperature of 20°C the difference in temperature between the water and the slab is higher, thus increasing the heat exchange. Consequently, despite the shorter cooling period, the cooling effect is almost identical to that when the room is cooled for 24 hours.

This clearly shows one of the advantages of using the concrete slab to store heat. The peak load obtained and stored during the day subsequently diminishes overnight. Consequently, the size of the cooling system can be kept small. Furthermore, it can be operated at night when the cost of electrical energy is lowest.

Concrete activation systems are often combined with ventilation systems which only need adjusting to supply the required air volume and provide an acceptable air quality. During the day, the cooling system is used to prepare the ventilation air; at night it is used to cool the concrete slab. Thus only a small cooling system is required.

As the system operates under dynamic conditions, it is rather difficult to determine the overall cooling-heating capacity. Capacity is calculated on the same basis as for radiant heating and cooling systems. The maximum capacity attained with concrete core activation is 20–30 W/m² for heating and 30–50 W/m² for cooling.

In office buildings, double floors are frequently used to accommodate cables. With concrete

activation systems, the greater part of the heat is conveyed to the underside – i.e. the ceiling side – of the slab, so that suspended ceilings are not a practical option. But as the ventilation system only has to provide enough air to ensure an acceptable air quality (i.e. an air-exchange rate of 1–2 hrs⁻¹ instead of 4–6 hrs⁻¹), smaller ducts can be used, thus obviating the need for suspended ceilings. In this case, both the air ducts and the supply and return water lines can be installed in the corridors between the office rooms. Dispensing with suspended ceilings also makes buildings shorter, which in turn means a significant reduc-

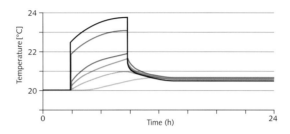

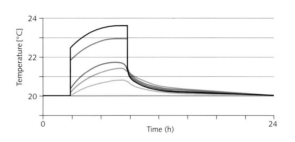

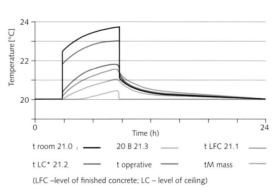

t room 21.0 | ——  20 B 21.3 ——  t LFC 21.1 ——
t LC* 21.2 ——  t operative ——  tM mass ——
(LFC –level of finished concrete; LC – level of ceiling)

The temperature in the "active" concrete core and the cooling period have a surprising effect on the operative temperature.

tion in construction and material costs. (Where suspended ceilings are no longer used, alternative solutions must be found to satisfy the requirements on sound insulation.)

### Regulation
With the radiant cooling system, it is important to limit surface and water temperatures low to avoid condensation. One approach is to make the minimum flow-water temperature dependent on the room's temperature at dew point, i.e. on its absolute humidity.

The result of a computer simulation in "degree hours" in which an operative temperature of 26°C is exceeded. The computations were carried out for different types of rooms and for rooms facing in different directions.

| | | West, light [°C x hrs] | East, light [°C x hrs] | West, heavy [°C x hrs] | East, heavy [°C x hrs] |
|---|---|---|---|---|---|
| Overall time | Without cooling | 14,600 | 14,600 | 13,600 | 13,600 |
| | 24 hr cooling | 360 | 400 | 0 | 0 |
| | 9 hr cooling | 1,320 | 1,600 | 560 | 800 |
| Time used | Without cooling | 3,200 | 4,000 | 3,000 | 3,600 |
| | 24 hr cooling | 0 | 0 | 0 | 0 |
| | 9 hr cooling | 360 | 520 | 160 | 360 |

Radiant heating and cooling systems are frequently combined with ventilation systems. In these combined systems, the air must be prepared to keep the incoming air temperature below that of the room air and to exclude any latent load due to dehumidification. This lowers humidity (the dew point), thus increasing the capacity of the radiant cooling system. Owing to their large storage mass, large storage units render individual regulation superfluous.

In most cases, zone control (north-south) is chosen, making it possible to regulate the flow-water temperature separately for each zone.

Typical of radiant heating and cooling systems are the relatively low temperature differences between surface and room. This allows for a great degree of self-regulation, since even a small difference in temperature has a great impact on the heat exchange between the cooled – or heated – surface and the room.

In a building with low heat and cold loads, concrete activation can be set at a constant water temperature for the entire year. If, for instance, the core temperature is kept constant at 22°C, the system will supply heat at temperatures below 22°C. Conversely, the system will begin cooling as soon as the room temperature exceeds 22°C.

### Energy Sources

Radiant or concrete core activation systems for heating and cooling buildings operate with relatively high cooling temperatures and relatively low heating temperatures. This creates better conditions for using renewable energy sources such as geothermal energy exchangers, aquifers and solar energy for heating and cooling, and for free cooling at night. The efficiency of heating boilers, refrigerating machines and heat pumps is likewise enhanced. In addition, a concrete-core activation system can be operated with night current, which is less expensive.

### Conclusions

Investigations show that these systems, operated in conjunction with carefully planned buildings, provide an interesting alternative to air-conditioning. As their heating and cooling capacity is limited, careful planning is necessary. They can only extract dry heat from a room. In order to extract latent heat as well, these systems are often combined with ventilation systems that exchange air. By permitting the use of smaller air-conditioning systems, these systems also provide greater overall comfort than fully air-conditioned rooms (noise, draughts). In addition, the absence of suspended ceilings means that buildings need not be so tall. Finally, since radiant heating and cooling systems operate with water temperatures close to room temperature, they create better conditions for using renewable energy sources and boost the efficiency of heating boilers, heat pumps and refrigerating machines.